CW00327051

VANCOUVER
& BRITISH COLUMBIA

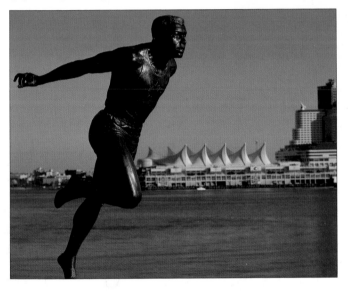

BY
CAROL BAKER

Produced by
Thomas Cook Publishing

Written by Carol Baker
Updated by Helena Zukowski

Original photography by Helena Zukowski
Original design by Laburnum Technologies Pvt Ltd

Editing and page layout by Cambridge Publishing
Management Ltd, Unit 2, Burr Elm Court,
Caldecote CB3 7NU
Series Editor: Karen Beaulah

Published by Thomas Cook Publishing
A division of Thomas Cook Tour Operations Ltd

PO Box 227, The Thomas Cook Business Park, Unit 18,
Coningsby Road, Peterborough PE3 8SB, United Kingdom
E-mail: books@thomascook.com
www.thomascookpublishing.com
Tel: +44 (0)1733 416477

ISBN-13: 978-1-84157-606-0
ISBN-10: 1-84157-606-9

Text © 2006 Thomas Cook Publishing
Maps © 2006 Thomas Cook Publishing
First edition © 2002 Thomas Cook Publishing
Second edition © 2006 Thomas Cook Publishing

Project Editor: Linda Bass
Production/DTP Editor: Steven Collins

Although every care has been taken in compiling this publication, and the contents are
believed to be correct at the time of printing, Thomas Cook Tour Operations Ltd cannot
accept any responsibility for errors or omissions, however caused, or for changes in details
given in the guidebook, or for the consequences of any reliance on the information provided.

The opinions and assessments expressed in this book do not necessarily represent those of
Thomas Cook Tour Operations Ltd.

Printed and bound in Spain by: Grafo Industrias Gráficas, Basauri

Cover design by: Liz Lyons Design, Oxford.
Front cover credits: Left © Peter Gridley, Getty Images; centre © Fotopic, Index Stock Imagery,
Photolibrary.com; right © Images MaXx, Index Stock Imagery, Photolibrary.com
Back cover credits: Left © britishcolumbiaphotos.com/Alamy; right © mediacolor's/Alamy

Contents

KEY TO MAPS

✈ Airport

● SkyTrain
   Station

³⁹⁵⁴ᵐ ▲ Mountain

☆ Start of walk/tour

(99A) Road number

• • Ferry route

Introduction

British Columbia, often referred to as BC, joined the Canadian Confederation in 1871, but is still regarded as a youngster in the world community. The life of this 'youngster', however, extends a long way back in time, to the creation of the majestic Coast Mountains, 130 million years ago. The north, with its extremes of temperature, is sparsely populated, while the urban centres of Vancouver and Victoria, where the climate is kind, are attracting more and more people all the time.

Jogging at Coal Harbour

The first residents were Asian hunters and berry gatherers, who drifted south along the coast and into the interior around 6000 BC. The first visitor to arrive by sea was probably Hoei-Shin, a Chinese Buddhist priest who sailed across the Pacific in AD 499.

Although Balboa claimed the Pacific Ocean and all its shores for Spain in 1513, the Spaniards did not settle here until the late 18th century. They stayed only a few years, but left their names: Cardero, Valdez, Juan de Fuca, Bodega y Quadra and Malaspina. Explorations by adventurers such as Captain Cook, Alexander Mackenzie, George Vancouver and Simon Fraser resulted in an influx of British settlers, and the area became a British colony in 1858.

Today, ironically, the Asians are back. More than 150,000 Chinese Canadians now live in BC. Other Chinese, both from Hong Kong and Taiwan, are investing in business, real estate and a new way of life in large numbers. The Japanese, who already own and manage many businesses in BC, also come by the jet-load on holidays, to marvel at the space, the wilderness, the native culture, and the slopes in Whistler, which they rate among the finest ski resorts of the world.

Vancouver, Canada's gateway to the Pacific, has become a wonderfully cosmopolitan centre, often blending the best of both European and Asian ways of life and, at the same time, encouraging a rebirth of BC's native Indian cultures.

'There's wine in the cup, Vancouver,
And there's warmth in my heart for you.'
Indian poetess Pauline Johnson, 1911

'Vancouver is one of those cities, like San
Francisco, which are victims of their
glorious settings. One expects too much of
them. As Californians like to say, there is
less to them than meets the eye.'
Travel writer Jan Morris, 1990

'I would not give the bleakest knoll on the
bleakest hill of Scotland, for all these
mountains in a heap.'
Explorer Captain John Gordon, 1844

'The history of Canada for about 300 years was a struggle to escape from the wilderness, and for the last half century has been a desperate attempt to escape into it.'
Canadian author Bruce Hutchison, 1953

'Every single time, when I come back to BC after a trip abroad, I thank my lucky stars I had the common sense to move here early enough in my life to truly appreciate the great natural beauty this province has to offer.'
Merchant banker Peter Thomas, 1991

'If I had known what it was like, I wouldn't have been content with a mere visit. I'd have been born here.'
Canadian humorist Stephen Leacock, 1937

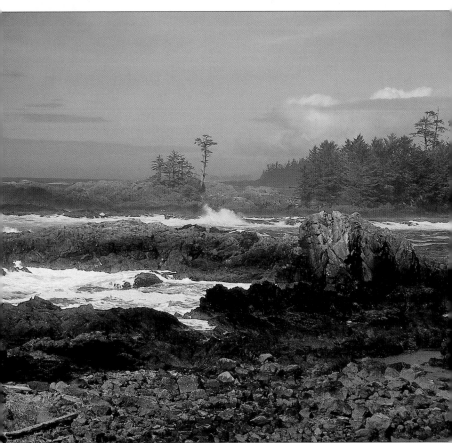

BC's wild Pacific coast

Land and people

The BC motto, *Splendor Sine Occasu*, which means 'splendour undiminished', is almost an understatement. Canada's most westerly province comprises 950,000 square kilometres of remarkably diverse seascapes and landforms – solitary beaches, quiet coves, primeval rainforests, spectacular fiords, snowcapped ranges, tundra, alpine meadows, glacial lakes, pristine waterfalls, rivers raging, and gentle, thermal springs, verdant valleys, plains and deserts.

An early BC resident, Royal BC Museum, Victoria

Geological past

About 130 million years ago, a gigantic upheaval in the earth's crust created the majestic Coast Mountains, the beginning of present-day BC. Sixty-five million years ago, further movements brought forth the Rocky Mountains, and 40 million years later, Cascadia, the Atlantis of the Pacific, sank offshore, leaving Vancouver Island and the Queen Charlotte Islands above sea level. A mere million years ago, most of BC was covered with a blanket of ice 2,500m (8,202 feet) thick, which slowly began to recede 70,000 years later.

At one time, a thick layer of ice pressed down over the region; its retreat about 10,000 years ago left the vast and visually delightful panorama of mountains, canyons, fiords, rivers and swamps. Without the weight of the ice, the land lifted, and layers of marine shells have been found several hundred metres above sea level.

All Fraser River delta land west of New Westminster developed after the ice retreated, and alluvial soils continue to create several metres of new real estate here every year.

A century ago, workers extending Granville Street unearthed ancient tools, weapons and ornaments in the Marpole Midden, the largest of its kind discovered in North America to that date. A similar midden in Stanley Park provided so many seashells, emptied and discarded by hungry native First Nations residents, that park roads were once paved with them.

Vancouverites received a reminder that the earth is alive in 1980, when Mount St Helens in Washington erupted and spewed a film of fine ash over the city. One of Vancouver's most famous landmarks, Siwash Rock in Stanley Park, is the uneroded remnant of a small volcano within the city limits, and black volcanic rock underpins nearby Prospect Point. Volcanic rock was quarried for road material out of the city highpoint that today is Queen Elizabeth Park. Mount Garibaldi, a short drive east, was an active volcano 1,000 years ago. Constant landslides onto mountain roads are a regular reminder that geological processes work without pause.

Vancouver has even had several minor earthquakes. One in 1946 registered 7.3 on the Richter scale at the epicentre, which was fortunately some distance north. But buildings rocked, and the big clock on the Vancouver Block stopped. Seismologists say Vancouver and its environs are very likely to feel the impact of 'The Big One', if and when it comes, although everyone prays that it won't.

Natural features

Each day, the sun sets over 6,500 islands, offshore from a rugged 12,000-km (7,456-mile) coastline indented by deep inlets. The magnificent Coast Mountains tower rank after rank in a northwest to southeast alignment. Eastward, a broad plateau of rolling rangeland, mantled with moraines and other glacial deposits, stretches towards the thrusting snowy peaks of the Rocky Mountains. These form a natural barrier between BC and the rest of Canada, which is accessible by land via mountain passes at Crowsnest, Kicking Horse and Yellowhead. Kimberly, located at an altitude of 1,100m (3,609 feet), is the highest city in the country. North of the Rockies stretch the extensive fertile farmlands of the

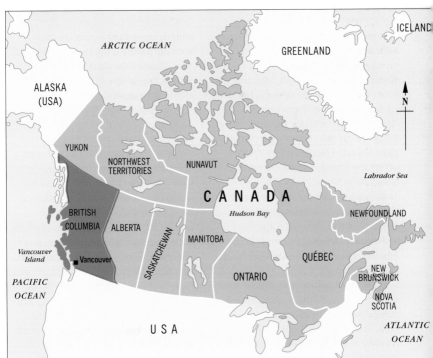

Peace River, a geographical continuation of the prairies.

The Fraser, Skeena, Nass, Stikine, Peace and Columbia rivers weave a web of routes and barriers throughout the province. The earth varies from the silty soil of the Fraser delta and the Okanagan Valley to the barren, lichen-covered lava fields of Terrace. Subterranean volcanic activity produces thermal springs at Harrison, Khalycon, Radium and Fairmont, which are open to the public for warm mineral baths.

Precipitation varies with topography, from the permanently damp rainforests of the Queen Charlotte Islands and frequent snowfalls of Mount Robson, the highest peak in the Rockies, to the sunny, arid Osoyoos desert with its cactuses, tumbleweed, sagebrush, lizards and rattlesnakes.

Taming the wilderness
Despite BC's vast and varied geography, man has made most areas accessible. A network of paved highways and railway tracks covers the countryside. The BC ferry fleet, the largest in the world, serves the islands and coastal towns, while in summer, luxury liners cruise to and from Alaska along the Inside Passage. International airports at Vancouver and Victoria, 350 other airfields and landing strips, and 100 seaplane bases permit access to remote regions.

Forestry and allied industries, which employ 80,000 British Columbians, face stiff pressure from increasing world competition which is eroding their traditional markets. Environmentalists, concerned over the future of the forests,

BC – the ultimate temperate rainforest

are alarmed at how the forests are being managed.

Although timber, mining, agriculture and fishing all contribute to provincial coffers, tourism brings in the most revenue. Visitors, who are mostly other Canadians, Americans and Japanese, usually stay longer in BC than anywhere else in the country.

What nature has created, mankind has complemented with almost every conceivable recreational facility, resulting in a remarkable playground, especially in summer. More than 300 land parks and 32 marine parks offer wilderness varying from the 30 alpine lakes and five glaciers of Kokanee Glacier Provincial Park to the colourful underwater world of anemones, abalone and other aquatic creatures sought out by scuba divers along the coast.

Weather
If grey skies and wet weather bother you, it is better to gamble on the drier and sunnier summer. From November to March, it is often dark and rainy.

About 250mm (10 inches) of rain drenches Vancouver in December, compared with 50mm (2 inches) in July. The thermometer hovers around 24°C (75°F) in July and around 6°C (43°F) in December. Vancouver snows tend to be light and melt quickly. Winter rain downtown often means snow on the nearby mountains, so skiers can ski all day and evening and still get back downtown for a nightcap. Cool Pacific breezes make seashore strolls pleasant in summer. Now that wood and coal no longer heat homes, there is less smog than there used to be, but an occasional patch of fog can slow drivers down in autumn. Although a less drastic version of Los Angeles smog lays a thin beige blanket over the city, most visitors find the air refreshing.

The climate is kind in Victoria and Vancouver. Resources are abundant.

Yet most of the wilderness remains wilderness.

The people

BC is a complexity of cultures. There has been an increasing variety of people coming to live in Vancouver during the past few decades, and the resulting mixture is exhilarating. Immigrants from Hong Kong, Taiwan, Japan, Vietnam and the Philippines in Asia, from Ethiopia, South Africa and Nigeria in Africa, from the USA, from many countries in Europe, and from Australasia have transformed the city. Everywhere, little neighbourhoods with a concentration of people from one culture keep popping up, and most of the world is represented in the restaurants offering international cuisine, and the shops selling souvenirs and objets d'art.

A mosaic of cultures in Vancouver

History

13 June 1792	Captain George Vancouver, exploring the Pacific Coast of North America, enters a body of water he names Burrard's Channel. Today, known as Burrard Inlet, it is the busy Vancouver harbour.
2 July 1808	Simon Fraser, seeking fur-trading routes, arrives at Musqueam at the mouth of the Fraser River, where the native people chase him and his men back upstream.
1846	After a long territorial dispute, a treaty is signed by Britain and the USA, placing BC firmly in Canada.
2 August 1858	Following the discovery of gold on the Fraser River, American miners begin to pour in. The British Parliament passes an act establishing the mainland colony of BC. The colony of Vancouver Island already exists.
25 November 1858	Colonel Richard Moody arrives with a company of 'sappers' (soldier engineers) and begins building roads. The first road built still exists, as

North Road, now the boundary between the Vancouver suburbs of Burnaby and Coquitlam.

26 September 1862	The McCleery family become the first settlers in Vancouver when they occupy land on the north bank of the Fraser River on what is now McCleery Golf Course.
October 1862	Three new arrivals from England, John Morton, Samuel Brighouse and William Hailstone, file a claim on 202 hectares (500 acres) on Burrard Inlet. The land is empty, swampy forest, so other colonists laughingly call them 'The Three Greenhorns'. Today, that land, the city's apartment-crammed West End, is worth billions.
June 1863	A sawmill, the first industry in the area, is established on the north shore of Burrard Inlet.
30 September 1867	'Gassy' Jack Deighton, so nicknamed because he talked incessantly, builds a saloon in 24 hours with the help of thirsty sawmill workers. The area

	around his saloon becomes known as Gastown.
1869–70	Gastown gets a jail . . . and the name Granville.
20 July 1871	BC joins the Confederation of Canada, formed in 1867.
6 April 1886	The City of Vancouver, renamed from Granville, is incorporated.
13 June 1886	The Great Fire destroys most buildings in the new little city, and 20 people die. Rebuilding begins at once.
23 May 1887	The first Canadian Pacific Railway (CPR) passenger train arrives in Vancouver; Vancouver's growth begins to accelerate.
1902	Vancouver's population reaches 30,000. Charles Woodward opens a department store, still active today.
1904	The Great Northern Railway reaches Vancouver.

1908	The University of BC is founded, which today has 30,000 students.
1913	The World Building is completed, the tallest in the British Empire at the time. Today, known as the Old Sun Tower, it looks rather modest.
28 August 1915	The first Canadian Northern Pacific Railway train arrives in Vancouver. Later, the line becomes known as the Canadian National Railway (CNR).

'Gassy' Jack Deighton

1 November 1919	The CNR Station opens. Today it is the terminal for VIA Rail.
1 January 1929	On amalgamation with two adjacent municipalities, Vancouver becomes Canada's third-largest city, with nearly one-quarter of a million people.
22 July 1931	Vancouver Airport and Seaplane Harbour officially open.
4 December 1936	Vancouver's City Hall opens.
25 May 1939	The third, and present, Hotel Vancouver opens on its present site, just a few days before King George VI and Queen Elizabeth stay there. The city names its newest park Queen Elizabeth Park.
6 August 1940	Theatre Under The Stars begins in Stanley Park, a much-loved tradition.
9 October 1944	The *St Roch*, a vessel operated by the Royal Canadian Mounted Police, arrives back in Vancouver from Halifax, having gone through the Northwest Passage in both directions. Shortly afterwards, the *St Roch* sails through the Panama Canal, becoming the first ship to circumnavigate North America.
15 July 1959	Queen Elizabeth and Prince Philip officiate at the opening of the Deas Island Tunnel, now called the Massey Tunnel.
10 September 1965	Simon Fraser University opens.
1986	EXPO 86, marking Vancouver's centennial, attracts 21 million visitors in six months and puts Vancouver in the spotlight around the world.
1996	New terminal opens at Vancouver International Airport.
6 April 2001	Vancouver celebrates turning 115 years old.
21 April 2001	Bjossa, the two-year-old female orca, moves from the Vancouver Aquarium to Sea World in San Diego, California. Bjossa was the last live killer whale left at the Aquarium, where she became a member in 1980.
23 January 2006	After eight years of Liberal government, the Conservative Party wins the general election.

BC and Canadian flags
flying on Burrard Street

Governance

Canada is a confederation with a parliamentary democracy. In the general election of January 2006, the Conservatives led by Stephen Harper gained enough votes to form a minority government, ending eight years of rule by the middle-of-the-road Liberal Party, headed by Jean Chretien.

BC's turbulent regional politics are a source of constant astonishment and amusement to the rest of the country (there are ten major provinces, of which BC is one, each of which having its own Premier, and two territories, one of which is administered by Inuit people).

From 1991 to 2001, the New Democrats held power. In 2000, Ujjal Dosanjh, an Indo-Canadian, replaced Glen Clark as the leader of the NDP and became Premier of BC. In May 2001, the Liberal Party won the provincial election and its leader, Gordon Campbell, a former Vancouver mayor, became Premier of the province. The ratio of women and of university graduates in local politics is the highest in BC history. Time will reveal the results these liberalising troops will have on the province's fortunes.

The province's lively political scene is reflected in microcosm in Vancouver, its largest city. For years, left-leaning members of the city council have been engaged in an ideological battle with the right, with middle-of-the-road councillors running the gauntlet. In the 2005 city elections, Sam Sullivan, a quadriplegic and active city councillor for years, replaced former mayor Philip Owen.

BC's 19th-century Parliament building

Culture and events

Vancouver plays host to a full programme of festivals, exhibitions, sporting events and other special celebrations. Most of them are concentrated in the summer, but there is hardly a month of the year when there isn't something special going on. For more information, contact Tourism Vancouver (*tel: (604) 683 2000; www.tourismvancouver.com*).

The HSBC Celebration of Light

In a vibrant city like Vancouver, some people work on Friday, ski on Saturday and sail on Sunday. Possibilities abound for the best in opera, art, theatre, music and cinema on a Saturday evening.

FESTIVALS AND SPECIAL EVENTS
Polar Bear Swim
January
Every New Year's Day more than 2,000 Vancouverites and visitors plunge into the chilly winter waters of English Bay.

Chinese New Year
End January/beginning February
A colourful celebration of old and modern traditions by Vancouver's Oriental community, highlighted by the Dragon Parade in Chinatown.

Vancouver Playhouse International Wine Festival
Various venues, late Feb/early March
Features 500 international wines.

The Cloverdale Rodeo
May
One of the largest rodeos on the continent, held at the fairgrounds over Victoria Day (24 May or preceding weekend).

Vancouver International Children's Festival
Vanier Park, May
A sea of candy-striped tents transforms the park into a wonderland of theatre, music, dance, puppetry, mime and acrobatics. Runners from all over the world compete in the **Vancouver International Marathon**.

Alcan Dragon Boat Festival
June
A weekend of racing and entertainment.

Vancouver International Jazz Festival
June
Big names in jazz perform at 40 venues in and around the city. Gastown has a two-day New Orleans-style street festival.

Bard on the Beach Shakespeare Festival
June–September
Different beach venues.

Canada Day
1 July
Entertainment and a spectacular fireworks show centred in Canada Place.

Dancing on the Edge Festival
July
A ten-day dance festival, centred on the Firehall Arts Centre.

Vancouver Folk Music Festival
July
Three days of performances by local and international singers, musicians and storytellers, at various venues.

Vancouver International Comedy Festival
July
Featuring a diverse collection of comic performers from around the world.

HSBC Celebration of Light
July
A spectacular international fireworks competition over English Bay.

Abbotsford Air Show
Abbotsford Airport, August
Aerial acrobatics, skydiving and wing-walkers fill the skies.

Pacific National Exhibition Concerts
August
Agricultural exhibitions and an amusement park take over the PNE Grounds for two weeks.

Air Canada Championship
Northview, August
This PGA tournament draws golfers from many countries.

The Fringe
September
Vancouver's theatre festival features 100 groups from around the world.

Vancouver International Film Festival
September
One of the country's best.

Mid-Autumn Moon Festival
October
A Chinese cultural celebration, including a lantern festival.
Traditional **Thanksgiving** celebrations take place at the Burnaby Village Museum (*tel: (604) 293 6501; www.burnabyparksrec.org*).

Festival of Lights
December
The central areas of VanDusen Gardens.

Christmas Carol Ship Parade
December
Greater Vancouver boat owners sail around the harbour in decorated craft.

Christmas at Canada Place
December
In support of local children's charities.

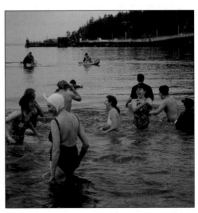
The annual Polar Bear Swim

Impressions

'You think BC means before Christ. But it doesn't. I'm sitting, wildly surmising, on the edge of the Pacific, gazing at mountains which are changing colour every two minutes in the most surprising way. Nature here is half-Japanese.'

English poet **Rupert Brooke**, 1913

An unusual way of getting around

What to bring

Vancouver has become such a meeting ground of east and west and of business and sports, that almost any wardrobe is acceptable on any occasion. Some women wear fox fur jackets and sandals to the office, while others wear parkas and running shoes. Shorts for both sexes are acceptable leisurewear in summer, but a sweater is often welcome after the sun sets over the Pacific. An umbrella, raincoat and water-resistant footwear can be useful any time of the year, but more so in winter. Layered clothes are

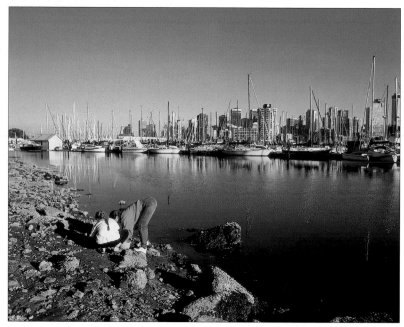

Coal Harbour, Vancouver

practical for trekking up the North Shore mountains or for boating. Don't worry if you haven't brought what you need, for practically everything is sold here. Clothes are generally more expensive than in the USA, but cheaper than in Europe.

Driving and parking

More than 80 per cent of the travellers

Get some exercise at False Creek, Vancouver

The Alienating

Mist rolls slowly back up the field
a retreating ghost army under
the mother-of-pearl-ringed moon
down the wide aisle of massed
trees ragged palisades of sheer
     darkness
jet against the prickling sky where
stars keep remote counsel beyond
the perimeters of the wind.

Unbending pioneers
wrestled this farm from the forest
broke the deathgrip of stumps
worried the sour dirt arable
danced often in that silvered-roofed
     barn
to the fiddle's plangent whine
whirled through squares and circles
when toil stung them hungry for
     frolic.

But this is a crueller night and time
we spin to more-cynical music
it hammers its city-spawned
     rhythms
against the ribs of the farmhouse
     behind me
I crouch in limbo beyond the
     window lights
a sudden stranger to both worlds
straining for the thoughts of Sascha
     the dog
and Friendly the sheep, chewing his
     slow dreams.

PETER TROWER

in BC are motorists. Driving is on the right, with passing on the left. The use of seatbelts is mandatory. Right turns are permitted on red lights, after the vehicle has come to a full stop. City streets, freeways and country roads are well maintained.

Vancouver is becoming more crowded. Rush hour seems to be getting longer and parking downtown more challenging. Many parking meters are restricted during rush hours. There are plenty of big parking lots indoors and out, but on busy days it may take a while to find a space. To Europeans, Vancouver drivers may seem almost archaically sedate, Victorians even more so, although driving manners appear to be deteriorating.

Vancouverites are often called 'Canada's eccentrics'

Local customs

Vancouver is an orderly city. People
usually queue patiently at bus stops and
taxi stands. Pedestrians use zebra
crossings, as they have the right of way
at intersections. Drivers rarely honk
their horns, a ticketable offence, even
when the traffic is reminiscent of
downtown Bangkok at rush hour. If you
ask for directions, remember that streets
are usually referred to by just the main
part of the name – 'Seymour Street' will
therefore be known as 'Seymour'.

Canadian couples are used to sleeping
in double beds, but many rooms have
two beds for the asking. Vancouverites
usually eat salads before the main course,
and green, Caesar and Greek salads are
very popular. BC now produces some
excellent wines so Vancouverites are

beginning to steer away from imported
wines in favour of BC labels.

Smoking on the street, once
considered bad form, is now common,
as most office buildings do not
permit smoking, even in lounge
areas. Please smoke in designated
areas only.

Some of the dour Scots who once
settled this area have left a legacy of
appearing unapproachable – or maybe it
is a remnant of the Wild West, where
any stranger was subject to suspicion.
Unlike their Seattle cousins,
Vancouverites seem reluctant to be the
first to say hello, although they usually
respond well to friendly people, and
though they pretend to be puritan at
times, the doorman at almost every
downtown hotel will accept a $5 tip and

keep your car nearby for you at no additional charge.

On the quiet, most residents of Vancouver admit their city is one of the most beautiful in the world. Few venture into the great outdoors during the dark, rainy days of winter, while others jog compulsively right through thunderstorms without losing pace. In the rain, it is a little easier to distinguish the locals; they're usually the ones without umbrellas.

Many visitors find the great patches of wilderness in Greater Vancouver, particularly on the North Shore, more than adequate for a short visit. But travellers seeking solitude may want to head into the hinterland, where the people are friendlier and nature's creations are unspoilt.

A Run Through Stanley Park
The cedar hand, wind nodded,
Caressed my arm and sought,
It seemed, my company.

For greeting or chastisement
At my ungreen intrusion?
Habit fit that path to pounding pace;

Yet these verdant curtains
May flail my fondness with fret
That I break the filtered, falling
  shaft

And sever
The thrust
Too rare in this soft scene.

BRUCE I BURNETT

The Wild Pacific Trail

Trendy people, trendy dogs – False Creek

Areas of Vancouver

Greater Vancouver is bounded by the North Shore mountains to the north, the Strait of Georgia to the west and the American border to the south. As more people move to the city, the fertile farmlands of the Fraser Valley to the east are fast being replaced by suburban development.

Downtown Vancouver

In addition to the main business and shopping area, the city centre has several different sections. Gastown, the renovated original part of the city, contains souvenir shops, restaurants and art galleries. **Robson Street** has several blocks of upmarket shops and restaurants with more of the same including high-end art galleries along South Granville Street. Chinatown has a colourful collection of shops and restaurants especially lively at weekends.

Yaletown is an area of old warehouses, recently renovated to house restaurants, galleries and studios of artists, architects and designers.

As a result of large-scale immigration, various ethnic enclaves have developed in Vancouver, and shops and restaurants have opened to cater to their tastes. There are also a lot of East Indians along the southern end of Main Street, Greeks along West Broadway, Germans on Fraser Street and Italians on Commercial Drive, and around Hastings and Nanaimo streets. There is a tiny Japantown on Powell Street and an equally small French-language pocket on West 16th Avenue.

The city's economic watershed is often held to be Cambie Street. To oversimplify, west of that north-south route live physicians, architects, business executives and college professors; east are sawmill workers, waitresses and factory workers.

Kerrisdale

Gentrification in recent years has polished the image of this neighbourhood, which is now smarter and shinier than Kitsilano to the north.

Kitsilano

Kitsilano, especially along West Fourth Avenue, was once a hotbed of the hippy era, with its pot smokers, tie-dyers, vegetarians, protesters and peaceniks. It still remains the most laid-back neighbourhood in town.

Shaughnessy

In this wealthy neighbourhood, streets lined with towering trees curve around imposing mansions. Shaughnessy was established by the Canadian Pacific Railway a century ago as a residential enclave for executives. In the poorest section, in downtown eastside with Hastings and Carrall streets as its hub, a committed group of residents is fighting to improve conditions.

Suburbia
Nearly two dozen suburbs surround Vancouver. **Richmond**, the site of Vancouver International Airport, is a rapidly growing city to the south. Surrey, a huge municipality on the south side of the Fraser River, is also expanding fast, partly due to the recent extension of the SkyTrain rapid transit. The southern part of **Surrey** is very attractive, with dairy farms dotted around the green, rolling hills.

A quiet, high-income, no-industry, residential area, West Vancouver has some of the most agreeable suburbs.

Downtown Vancouver

AREAS OF BC

The Rockies

This region stretches northwest from the 49th parallel along the Alberta border. The main highway follows the Columbia River through the broad valley of the Rocky Mountain Trench.

Cariboo Chilcotin

This region stretches from the fiords of the Pacific to the forested foothills of the Cariboo mountains.

High Country

This vast region offers lakes and rivers, glaciated mountain passes, waterfalls, forests and arid desert plateaux.

Kootenay Country

This region nestles between the fertile farmlands of the Okanagan Similkameen and the Rockies.

North by Northwest

This vast area encompasses one-third of BC and stretches from the Rockies to Haida Gwaii (the Queen Charlotte Islands).

Okanagan Similkameen

This small, L-shaped region is situated along the American border midway between the Rockies and the Pacific. The Okanagan Valley produces much of the province's wines.

Peace River–Alaska Highway

This region is set between the foothills of the Rockies and the Alberta prairie. The Alaska Highway runs from Dawson Creek (Mile Zero) northwest through Fort Nelson and Liard Valley to Alaska.

British Columbia

Vancouver

Vancouver, commonly called the Gateway to the Pacific, is almost entirely surrounded by water. To the north is Burrard Inlet, an ice-free harbour where freighters fly flags from many nations. To the south, the Fraser River flows west into the Strait of Georgia, which separates Vancouver and the rest of the mainland from Vancouver Island. As a prairie farmer remarked, 'Vancouver would be great, if the view wasn't blocked by the mountains'. The sheltering ranges attract grey clouds that shower the city with 140cm (55 inches) of rain a year, resulting in fresh air and lush green landscapes. The clouds frost the peaks with snow for city skiing five months a year.

Mounties are everywhere!

Metropolitan Vancouver covers 3,000sq km (1,158sq miles), including the suburbs of North Vancouver, West Vancouver, Burnaby, Coquitlam, Port Coquitlam, Port Moody, Pitt Meadows, Richmond, White Rock, Delta, New Westminster, Surrey and Langley.

Although Vancouver is Canada's third-largest city (after Toronto and Montreal), the many waterways, mountains and parks lend the illusion of space.

While the past has been largely the story of seeking and selling natural resources, new industries are emerging. Local skills now produce sightseeing submarines, satellite-sensing equipment, computer software and data terminal designs.

A growing tourism industry draws some visitors back as residents. Hotels continue to spring up in a city centre of skyscrapers. Well-developed facilities and roadways allow visitors and residents to ski in the morning, sail in the afternoon and enjoy opera in the evening. Even business seems a sport in this city, which has one of the most speculative stock markets in the world.

Most people come to Vancouver for the scenery, so first select one of its many vantage points for an overview of the city. People who like to keep their feet firmly planted on the ground may prefer to stroll along the promenade deck at Canada Place, a good orientation spot. With its five white sails jutting out into the harbour, this city landmark features a dozen markers indicating sites of interest around the city. You can also enjoy spectacular views from the air or from downtown city buildings. Another great way to orient yourself is to take an aerial tour and get a real bird's-eye view.

Aerial sightseeing
Harbour Air
BC's largest seaplane company packages 18 tours, varying from a half-hour flight over the city centre to a six-hour round trip to Vancouver Island.
Tel: (604) 274 1277, toll free (800) 665 0212; www.harbour-air.com

Pegasus Ballooning Ltd
Enjoy the ultimate romantic adventure – aloft with the breeze over the verdant Fraser Valley, followed by a traditional champagne celebration upon landing.
24202 56th Ave, Langley.
Tel: (604) 533 2701.

Helijet
Scenic city and wilderness tours, departing from downtown and Grouse Mountain. Options range from a 20-minute flight over English Bay, Stanley Park and the Lions Gate Bridge, to the two-hour Mountain Odyssey, with a 20-minute stopover on a glacier.
5911 Airport Rd South, Richmond.
Tel: (604) 270 1484;
toll free (800) 665 4354; www.helijet.com

Bird's-eye viewpoints
Cloud Nine
The price of a meal or a drink at the Cloud Nine restaurant, atop the 42-storey Empire Landmark Hotel, includes a 360-degree view of Vancouver.
1400 Robson St. Tel: (604) 687 0511.

Harbour Centre
The glass elevators on the south side of Harbour Centre rise 167m (548 feet) to The Lookout! cafeteria, a revolving restaurant and viewing deck, which features a 30-minute video about Vancouver.
555 West Hastings St. Tel: (604) 689 0421; www.vancouverlookout.com
Open: daily 9am–9pm.
Admission charge.

Vistas on the Bay
Gourmets of both food and scenery love the revolving Vistas restaurant at the top of the Renaissance Hotel.
1133 West Hastings St. Tel: (604) 689 9211. Viewing free.

The view from the top of the Harbour Centre

The charm of BC's beaches

Vancouver's beaches are an essential part of the city's outdoor culture. They provide the perfect venue for cycling, rollerblading, beach volleyball, or, on a more relaxing note, a romantic stroll, and, of course, sunbathing.

On New Year's Day in Vancouver, however, around 2,000 locals dash into English Bay for the Polar Bear Swim. No one lingers long; they dress quickly and head indoors to recuperate from the chilling waters.

But summer is another story. Beaches become crowded with swimmers, sand-castle builders, frisbee players, kite flyers and sunseekers who want to do exactly nothing. An occasional canine slips in without permission, and squirrels sometimes appear hoping for handouts. Towards sunset, an entrepreneur with a metal detector in hand may sift the sands hoping for hidden treasures.

Although many people bring picnics, alcohol is not allowed; but it is rumoured that every now and then a thermos brings in wine masquerading as Kool-Aid. There are sandy, gravel and pebble shores. English Bay's Sunset Beach is ribboned with gigantic trunks from rainforest trees that escaped log booms, a reminder that timber is a key industry here. The logs are great for leaning on, and they provide some privacy. Some are big enough for a single sunbather to stretch right out on top.

Although the sun is tempered by refreshing offshore breezes, it is wise to wear a strong sunscreen for protection against the direct rays and those reflected off the sea and sand. West

Vancouver's Ambleside Beach is one of the few city beaches to permit electric barbecues. It is wonderful to roast hot dogs and marshmallows around a flickering fire as the Lions Gate Bridge lights up and the sunset fades into the darkening evening sky over English Bay.

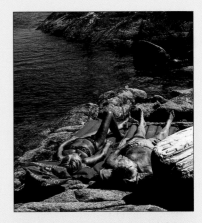

The beaches around the city provide idyllic recreational spaces for urbanites

Beaches

Although beachcombing is a pleasant pastime come rain or shine in winter, Vancouver beaches are at their best in summer. From Victoria Day to Labour Day, lifeguards supervise the city's ten swimming beaches from 11.30am to 9pm. There is no admission charge to the beaches, and changing rooms, toilets and refreshment stands are found in many convenient locations.

Kitsilano Beach

English Bay (First Beach)
Fifteen minutes from downtown Vancouver, English Bay sports several fine beaches.
At the foot of Davie & Denman Sts.

Kitsilano Beach
Kitsilano Beach has a heated outdoor saltwater pool overlooking that great unheated 'pool', English Bay. Nearby Jericho Beach, Locarno Beach and Spanish Banks are favourites with windsurfers. There is adequate parking, there are plenty of interesting food stalls, and picnic tables are scattered along the beach.
Southwest of the Burrard St Bridge.

Second Beach
This beach features a pool that protects children from the currents. There are areas for picnics and barbecues and for playing soccer, football, volleyball and baseball.
In Stanley Park, north of Sunset Beach.

Sunset Beach
At this beach, the closest to downtown, summer sunsets are glorious. Residents and visitors congregate on giant logs on the beach or sip sundowners at the front tables in the nearby English Bay Café and the Sylvia Hotel to contemplate the end of another day.
At the corner of Pacific Ave & Jervis St.

Third Beach
This isolated beach is relatively quiet, a haven for those looking to get away from the metropolitan crush.
On the west side of Stanley Park, north of Second Beach & Ferguson Point.

Wreck Beach
This beach has unrivalled natural beauty. A steep trail (not easy to find, ask for directions) winds down to the water from North West Marine Drive to this unspoilt wild strand, the only nudist beach in the Lower Mainland.
On the tip of the Point Grey peninsula near the University of British Columbia (UBC).

For information, contact Kits Tower in season (tel: (604) 738 8535); and Vancouver Aquatic Centre, off season (tel: (604) 665 3424); www.city.vancouver.bc.ca/parks/rec/ beaches

Colourful signs,
Chinatown

Chinatown

Vancouver's thriving Chinatown, a 10-minute walk from the city centre, stretches over six blocks, north to south from Main Street to the Georgia Street viaduct, and east to west from Gore Street to Carrall Street. Millions of dollars change hands here, in hundreds of businesses ranging from banks to food to electronics. Chinese immigrants bring in an estimated $2 billion to BC every year.

Chinatown is home to a few thousand permanent residents, mostly elderly. Most Chinese Canadians live elsewhere, but come to Chinatown to bank, shop and eat. The streets bustle with activity. Shops overflowing with rosewood furniture, bamboo and wickerware, jade jewellery and porcelain stand cheek-by-jowl with herbal pharmacies and authentic Chinese restaurants, most of which serve excellent food at reasonable prices.
For more information:
www.vancouver-chinatown.com

Chinese Cultural Centre

Situated between Carrall and Columbia streets (*see p30*), the Chinese Cultural Centre houses changing exhibitions of traditional culture and local history and sponsors the annual Chinese New Year Parade.
50 East Pender St. Tel: (604) 658 8850;
www.cccvan.com. Open: Tue–Wed
9am–9pm, Thur–Sun 9am–5.30pm.
Closed Mon. Free admission.

Dr Sun Yat-Sen Park and Garden

This garden (*see p30*), opened for Expo 86, was created in classical Chinese style

and is a harmonious blend of plants and space, with numerous terraces, pavilions and walkways.
578 Carrall St. Tel: (604) 662 3207.
Hours vary according to season. Call for current opening times. Admission charge.

Sam Kee Building

See p30.
At the southwest corner of Pender &
Carrall sts. Not open to the public, but can be viewed from outside.

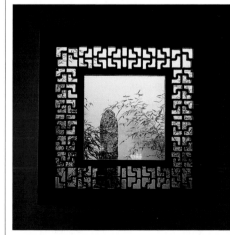

Window at the Dr Sun Yat-Sen Park

Walk: Chinatown

Vancouver's Chinatown (*see also p29*), the second largest in North America (at present) after San Francisco, crams a lot of life into six city blocks, a 10-minute walk from the city centre.

Allow 2 hours for walking and another hour for dim sum (*see pp166–7*).

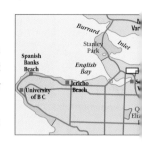

Begin this tour at the southwest corner of Carrall and Pender sts.

1 Sam Kee Building

Built in 1913, the Sam Kee Building is the narrowest building in the world (1.8m by 30m/6 feet by 98 feet), and is listed in the *Guinness Book of Records*. The two-storey building, once living quarters for a Chinese family, is now home to Jack Chow Insurance and a group of architects upstairs who own the building.

2 Chinese Cultural Centre

In the next block east, the Chinese Cultural Centre, marked by an enormous red gateway, houses a library and rooms for language lessons, *tai chi*, Chinese painting, lantern making and frequently changing exhibits of Oriental and Canadian art.

Behind the CCC lies the Dr Sun Yat-Sen Park and Garden.

3 Dr Sun Yat-Sen Park and Garden

High, whitewashed walls hide this pocket of peace from the bustling city beyond. Modelled after the classic scholars' gardens of the Ming Dynasty (1368–1644), the Taoist balance of yin and yang (light and shadow, smooth and rough, large and small) creates perfect harmony. This quiet, secluded sanctuary shelters varied vistas of pebbled patios, moon gates, lattice windows, see-through shrubbery, placid milky-jade pools and craggy grey limestone.

Cross Pender St.

4 Pender Street

Across Pender Street, the Wing Sang Building, housing the Yen Lock Restaurant, is the oldest structure in Chinatown, dating from 1889.

Both sides of Pender are lined with Mandarin, Cantonese and Szechuan restaurants, and shops selling such imported goods as wickerware, parasols, porcelain, bamboo birdcages and jade jewellery. Prices are reasonable, and browsers are welcome. At the Chinese pharmacies, you can see experts mixing potions of herbs, ginseng root, dried cuttlefish, powdered antler velvet and other exotic ingredients for infusions to alleviate everything from influenza to impotence. Many Westerners now take ginseng and royal jelly.

Continue east along Pender St.

5 Little Japan

At 173 East Pender, down a few stairs, is Yeu Hua Crafts Ltd, specialists in arts and crafts from China. Their business card says 'wholesale welcome', so prices are probably negotiable, even though they sound reasonable. The store stocks a great selection of attractive rosewood furniture in various sizes, delicate porcelain and cloisonné, silk embroidery and paper goods. And Yeu Hua will ship everything home for you.

Cross Main St, still on Pender St, turn right on Gore Ave, walk a block to Keefer St and turn right again.

6 Keefer Street

Here, the predominant aroma announces windows of Chinese pastries. Most pastry shops have a room at the back for a tasty cup of tea and a snack (the coffee is usually mediocre). On the south side of Keefer stands a shopping centre, with Hon's Wun-tun House (great soup and noodles for low prices; cash only, no alcohol) at street level. As it happens, the big supermarket in the basement is not nearly as much fun as street shopping.

Follow Keefer St two blocks west back to the Dr Sun Yat-Sen Park and Garden.

Nearby
Church of China, Sun Tower

The Dr Sun Yat-Sen Garden, a taste of the Orient in Vancouver's Chinatown

During the 5th century, several Chinese Buddhist priests visited a country they called Fu Sang, now believed to have been the west coast of Canada. But the first real wave of Chinese immigrants did not arrive until the 1858 gold rush. Some stayed and started farms and laundries, or worked in the salmon canneries, sawmills and coal mines. Some 25 years later, 10,000 Chinese workers were imported to lay tracks for the cross-Canada railway. Racism forced Chinese families to live crowded together in a small area, the beginning of today's Chinatown in Vancouver. Now more than 332,560 Chinese Canadians live in Metropolitan Vancouver and others have settled elsewhere in the province.

Although 50 per cent of newcomers to BC are from other Canadian provinces, about 22,000 Asian immigrants are estimated to arrive each year. Most of the people arriving from Hong Kong and Taiwan bring considerable wealth, skills, willingness to work and sophistication.

Some Chinese come here because they like the space, the cleanliness, the order and the economic opportunities. Many Hong Kong families, concerned about Hong Kong's return to China in 1997, sent their teenage offspring to study in Canadian schools and universities, to provide them with more career opportunities. Others are investing capital in property, manufacturing, electronics and other ventures in BC so that they might take up residence here in the future.

Fortunately, the descendants of the original British settlers in BC are developing greater tolerance of other races. About 25 per cent of children entering school here speak Cantonese or Mandarin as their mother tongue, and young Vancouverites are no longer concerned whether their friends come from an Asian or European background. The highest office in the province, that of lieutenant-governor, was held, until recently, by David Lam, a highly respected and admired Chinese immigrant.

For more information contact the Chinese Cultural Centre, *tel: (604) 658 8880; www.cccvan.com*

Glimpses of Vancouver's thriving Chinatown

Walk: Gastown

Gastown, a five-minute hike from the city centre, is the oldest part of Vancouver. The area was designated a heritage site in 1971. Old gas-style lamps and young maple trees line cobblestoned Water Street, whose three blocks comprise the heart of Gastown. For more information visit *www.gastown.org*

Allow at least 2 hours.

Begin this tour at the corner of Richards and Water sts. Head east on the north side of Water St.

1 The Landing

The first stop, The Landing, is an award-winning heritage structure containing a dozen elegant shops clustered around a central lobby, whose arched floor-to-ceiling window frames the North Shore mountains. A shiny escalator leads from one polished oak floor to the other. Head to the lower level, pick up a local newspaper or the *New York Times* at the Fleet Street news-stand, and savour a cappuccino and muffin, a good melange of America and Europe, at the adjacent friendly café or the 1950s-style diner at the east end of the building.

Landmark shops sell Scottish tartans, Belgian chocolates, Japanese lingerie, cut and potted flowers, Canadian winter clothes, gold jewellery handcrafted on site, designer clothes, toys for children, embroidered Victoria cushions, maple-wood salad bowls and smoked salmon packed for shipping.

Continue along Water St.

2 Inuit Gallery

Water Street is lined with dozens of shops selling everything from souvenir sweatshirts to Art Deco furniture. The most exciting stop is the Inuit Gallery, a few doors east of The Landing, which houses an impressive array of Inuit sculpture and Northwest native art. The so-called naive art recalls the way Inuit families used to live in harmony with their harsh land, expressed in soapstone and whalebone sculptures.

The shop also sells Northwest native Canadian cedar carvings, buttoned blankets and ceremonial masks.
A little further along on the left is the steam clock.

3 Steam Clock

Dedicated to the citizens of Vancouver in 1977, the 2-ton steam clock was built by Gillett & Johnston of Croydon, England. The movement was based on an 1875 vintage design, and has a 19-kg (42-pound) gold-plated pendulum.

A machine in a nearby basement is triggered by clockwork every 15 minutes, and little pins play a Westminster Chimes tune which electronically blows five steam whistles. The steam manifold for the whistles sits on top of the cube housing the four dials, each highlighted by four enamelled copper dogwood flowers. A 24-carat gold-plated frame surrounds the dials which glow at night.
Continue along Water St.

4 The Courtyard

In the next block meander through The Courtyard where Vancouver architects, tour operators and lawyers work behind huge glass windows. The outdoor café and delicatessen up the stairs provides a pleasant pause with a view across the harbour.
At the end of Water St, turn right into Carrall St.

5 Maple Tree Square

In Maple Tree Square stands the statue of 'Gassy' Jack Deighton, a garrulous Yorkshireman who built a saloon for lumber mill workers on the site of the Broghes building behind in 1867. The

building is made with bricks from China that were used as ballast on sailing ships calling for timber at the Hastings Mill. Deighton, who had arrived in Vancouver with his wife, six dollars, a few sticks of furniture and a yellow dog, was an overnight success. Because he was so talkative and optimistic about prospects for Burrard Inlet, locals called him 'Gassy Jack', and the ramshackle collection of huts and shops surrounding the saloon was dubbed Gastown. The name stayed, although the city grew westward and changed its name to Vancouver. Jack's statue faces the old Europe Hotel, a good example of the renovated Victorian buildings in Gastown.
Turn west through the Gaoler's Mews.

6 Gaoler's Mews

This cobblestoned courtyard is where Vancouver's first gaol once stood. A little further along, Blood Alley marks the site of many dastardly deeds during the settlement of the Wild West.

The south side of Water Street is also lined with shops and restaurants. Water Street restaurants cover the cuisines of Italy, France, Kenya, India and America. One of the best stops for lunch is Umberto's Al Porto, whose downstairs replicates a Tuscan farmhouse and whose upstairs provides a panoramic sweep of railcars carrying Canadian wheat and containers, backdropped by helicopters landing at the heliport in front, and the SeaBus shuttling back and forth to North Vancouver.
Return along Water St to The Landing.

Nearby
Portside Park, Vancouver Vocational Institute

Trolley tour: Gastown to Chinatown

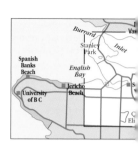

The Trolley Tour is the best preview of Vancouver's varied attractions. The four bright red-and-gold non-polluting gas-operated trolleys, decorated in oak and brass, are replicas of those used in the 1890s. Start in historic Gastown. You may jump off and explore at any of the 16 stops and then catch the next trolley.

Allow at least 2 hours.

1 Steam Clock
See p35.
The trolley travels northwest along

cobblestoned Water St past the old CPR Station, now the SeaBus terminal, to Canada Place.

2 Canada Place
Soaring canvas sails identify Canada Place, the city convention centre and cruise-ship berth for some of the most luxurious craft in the world.

3 Vancouver Tourist InfoCentre
Stop here to stock up on brochures about local attractions and events.

The tour wheels past the Vancouver Art Gallery on Hornby St and Robson Street's elegant restaurants and boutiques. It then follows Georgia St to Coal Harbour.

4 Coal Harbour
Look out for gaggles of Canada geese and float planes skimming forests of masts in the marina as they take off for Vancouver Island.
Further on, getting to Stanley Park, which juts out into English Bay, there are three interesting stops.

5 Totem Poles
A stunning array of native carvings, against a breathtaking view across Coal Harbour to Canada Place.

6 Aquarium
Canada's largest, it has belugas, otters and other aquatic residents.

7 Rose Garden
Enjoy the colour and breathe in the fragrance of 300 species of roses.
From here the trolley heads southwest through the densely populated West End.

8 West End
A cluster of skyscrapers looking across English Bay and Georgia Strait.
The route crosses the Burrard St Bridge to Chestnut St.

9 Vancouver Museum and Planetarium
Houses a huge array of artefacts which illustrate the West Coast settlement.

10 Granville Island
Decaying warehouses have been transformed into an area of theatres, art galleries, shops, restaurants, walkways and an indoor market.
The route follows Granville St and 33rd Ave to the edge of Queen Elizabeth Park to another converted warehouse area.

11 Yaletown
Now the trendiest address in town, Yaletown houses fashionable shops, cafés, pubs and galleries.
The trolley now heads downtown again, pausing first at City Hall.

12 City Hall
An Art Deco building built in 1936.
Passing by the Vancouver Public Library and Sports Hall of Fame, the trolley stops next at Science World.

13 Science World
A sparkling, 17-storey geodesic sphere built for EXPO 86, which is a hands-on science museum with one of the largest OMNIMAX theatres in the world.
On to Chinatown in Sun Yat-Sen Gardens. There are extra boarding stops at a number of downtown hotels.

14 Chinatown
Outdoor displays of exotic fruits and vegetables, and shop windows crowded with rattan, bamboo and brass.
The tour ends back at the steam clock in Gastown.

Tours run from 9am–4pm at 30-minute intervals from Apr–Oct. The last tour leaves Gastown at 4pm and returns at 6pm (tel: (604) 801 5515; fax: (604) 801 5557; toll-free (1 888) 451 5581; www.vancouvertrolley.com).

The gold-framed Steam Clock

Nature has been and continues to be the dominating influence motivating local artists. It is clearly evident in their work, from the powerful and mysterious moods of old-growth rainforests and totem poles painted by Emily Carr to the subtle watercolour seascapes of Toni Onley.

Emily Carr, born in Victoria in 1871, is acknowledged as the grand matriarch of BC art. Her inspiration came from both the natural surroundings and the original inhabitants, as she travelled the BC coast collecting and portraying a wealth of impressions from First Nations peoples, their arts and their legends.

Other BC greats include Bill Reid, Reg Davidson and Roy Vickers, who all have a native heritage; European immigrants John Coerner from the former Czechoslovakia, and Bratsa Bonisacho from the former Yugoslavia; Attila Rick Lukacs, originally from Alberta; as well as other talents such as Ross Penhall and Lorraine Yabuki.

Since the 1980s, local artists have

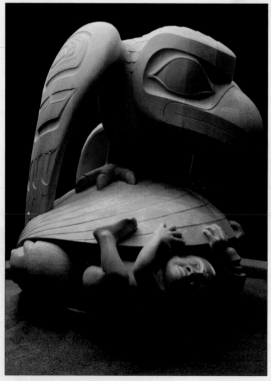

expressed a strong commentary on preserving the environment and on controversies focused around fishing, logging and endangered species.

The work of local photographers Jeff Wall, Rodney Graham, Fred Douglas and Marion Penner-Bancroft has earned international renown. And sculptors Roland Brennen and Mowry Baden, using plastics, electronics and other present-day products, have set a new direction for West Coast sculpture with their kinetic creations.

In addition to showing the contemporary works of resident painters, sculptors and photographers, local galleries hold regular exhibitions. These include First Nations' cedar carvings and paintings, with their traditional colourful oval designs, Inuit soapstone sculptures from the Arctic, as well as works by the Canadian Group of Seven (*www.groupofsevenart.com*) where Emily Carr was Associate Contemporary Artist, and old European and Asian masters.

Facing page: *The Raven and the First Men* by Bill Reid; above: Vancouver Art Gallery; right: Public art at Coal Harbour

Galleries

Vancouver is a young city, and youthful energy and enthusiasm are reflected in the freshness of its art scene, both in traditional West Coast art and in more avant-garde work. Since galleries often close to mount new shows and because some are staffed by volunteers, it is often wise to phone ahead to check opening times.

Public art can be found throughout the city

Downtown
Buschlen-Mowatt Gallery
Dedicated to showcasing museum-quality contemporary artists of regional, national and international significance, with a focus on sculpture.
1445 West Georgia St. Tel: (604) 682 1234; www.buschlenmowatt.ca
Dôrian Rae Collection
Asian and African art and artefacts.
410 Howe St. Tel: (604) 874 6100.
Rendez-vous Gallery
Located opposite the Four Seasons Hotel, the gallery sells paintings, prints and sculptures by emerging and established Canadian artists.
671 Howe St. Tel: (604) 687 7466; www.rendez-vousartgallery.com
Teck Gallery
Features changing exhibitions.
*Simon Fraser University, Harbour Centre, 505 West Hastings St.
Tel: (604) 681 5881.*
Vancouver Art Gallery
A Neoclassical heritage building and a work of art itself, it houses paintings by the early 20th-century Canadian artists known as the Group of Seven; evocative rainforest works by Emily Carr (1871–1945); works by Dutch, Italian, French, German and English masters;

and photography, sculpture, graphics and video works.

You can wander around on your own or join a free 20-minute tour. The reference-only library, gift shop and restaurant make the Vancouver Art Gallery a rainy-day special.
750 Hornby St. Tel: (604) 662 4719 for 24-hour information; www.vanartgallery.bc.ca

Gastown
Marion Scott Gallery
Features Inuit sculptures, prints, drawings and wall hangings.
308 Water St. Tel: (604) 685 1934.
Images For A Canadian Heritage
A good assortment of Inuit soapstone and whalebone sculpture, Northwest native woodcarvings, finely crafted silver jewellery and argillite sculptures. Other works in marble, bronze, glass and ceramics are also for sale.
164 Water St. Tel: (604) 685 7046; www.imagesforcanada.com
Inuit Gallery
Exhibits and sells excellent traditional Inuit masterworks, Cape Dorset Inuit sculpture and West Coast native Indian works.
206 Cambic St. Tel: (604) 688 7323.

Granville Island
Charles H Scott Gallery
Located in the Emily Carr Institute of Art and Design, the gallery mounts travelling shows. You can walk through the school and look at students' work.
1399 Johnston St, Granville Island. Tel: (604) 844 3809.
Lattimer Gallery
Sells many current works by First Nation artists.
1590 W 2nd Ave. Tel: (604) 732 4556; www.latimergallery.com

On Johnston Street beside the Creek House is Bill Reid's brilliant bronze sculpture, *The Spirit of Haida Gwaii*, which comprises a dozen characters of the Haida legend in a big canoe. First Nations guides provide complimentary commentary daily from 9am to 7pm. Bill Reid's studio can be visited by appointment (*tel: (604) 264 4880*).

South Granville
Alexander Harrison Galleries
Specialises in contemporary works of Canadian and European art.
2932 Granville St. Tel: (604) 732 5217.
Atelier Gallery
Sells contemporary art.
2421 Granville St. Tel: (604) 732 3021.
Bau-Xi Gallery
Features Canadian contemporary art. Be sure to look upstairs as well.
3045 Granville St. Tel: (604) 733 7011.
Catriona Jeffries
Exhibits and sells interesting contemporary local and imported art.
3149 Granville St. Tel: (604) 736 1554.
Diane Farris Gallery
Contemporary painting and sculpture from up-and-comers to established artists.
1590 W 7th Ave. Tel: (604) 737 2629; www.dianefarrisgallery.com
Equinox Gallery
Features international contemporary shows.
2321 Granville St. Tel: (604) 736 2405.
Petley Jones
Features contemporary and older works in dealer's stock.
2235 Granville St. Tel: (604) 732 5353.

Other galleries
Federation of Canadian Artists
Juried exhibits of original paintings by Canadian artists.
1241 Cartwright St. Tel: (604) 681 8534.
Western Front
The premier parallel gallery in Canada, with artist-managed gallery space.
303 E 8th Ave. Tel: (604) 878 7563.
Surrey Art Gallery
An eclectic programme of temporary exhibitions alongside its permanent collection.
13750 88th Ave, Surrey. Tel: (604) 501 5566.
Canoe Pass Gallery
Represents gifted Canadian native artists.
115–3866 Bayview Pier in Steveston. Tel: (604) 272 0095.

Statue (and friend) in Stanley Park

Walk: art in public places

Vancouver has a young but flourishing arts scene, and a great variety of interesting art in public places.
Allow about 2 hours.

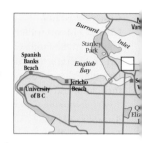

Begin at the Royal Bank of Canada at 1025 Georgia St.

1 Royal Bank of Canada

At the top of the escalator in the main lobby is the *Ksan Mural*. The nine panels of this 35-m (115-foot) long masterpiece in glowing red cedar, outlined in red, black and turquoise, depict the exploits of the raven in native Canadian mythology. The mural was created by six carvers from 'Ksan' (which means 'between the banks'), a native village reconstructed near Hazelton, on a site which has been in existence for over 7,000 years.
Continue east along Georgia St.

2 Cathedral Place

At Cathedral Place, 925 West Georgia, take time to watch the tinkling brass pipes and fractured glass of *Navigational Device* respond to the movement of people present in the foyer. This imposing sculpture, created by local artist Robert Studer, is based on a navigation aid found in the Queen Charlotte Islands. The hieroglyphics etched on the glass resemble Oriental language characters but are cryptic.
Turn right on Hornby St and walk south to Smythe. Turn left one block and then left down Howe St to Robson Sq.

3 Joy of Freedom

A bronze abstract by Geert Maas, a Dutch artist who lives in BC, was donated to BC in honour of all Canadians who contributed to the liberation of the Netherlands in 1944–5.
Continue walking northeast to the Vancouver Art Gallery.

4 Bird of Spring
This simplified bird-form sits on the stairs down to the plaza off Howe Street. The sculpture is a bronze replica of a 14-cm (5^1/$_2$-inch) original by Abraham Etungat, a Cape Dorset artist.

5 Spring
This red steel coiled spring appears to hold up the second level of the plaza.
Continue north to Georgia and Howe.

6 Hong Kong Bank of Canada
The next stop is the Hong Kong Bank of Canada at 885 West Georgia. The impulse to duck is almost irresistible as a 30-m (98-foot) long shining pendulum swings smoothly through the air just 4m (13 feet) overhead. The pendulum, sculpted by British Columbian Alan Storey, seems to form the workings of some wonderful stylised clock. The atrium café is a pleasant place to enjoy a cappuccino while contemplating the soothing rhythm of the giant pendulum.

Right across the street is a fabulous fountain, framed by the elegant columns and sweeping steps of the Vancouver Art Gallery, designed as a courthouse in 1907 by Victoria architect Francis Rattenbury. The fountain was built in 1966 to commemorate the union of the crown colonies of BC and Vancouver Island.
Walk one block north on Howe and turn left on Dunsmuir. Turn right on Hornby.

7 British Columbia beginning
A modern abstraction in golds, browns and reds in the Canadian Imperial Bank of Commerce tells BC's story.
Walk a block north and just beyond Pender Street to the TD Bank building.

8 BC Pageant
A pageantry mural representing early development in the province.
Continue to Hastings Street and turn left to Burrard. Turn right on Burrard, then right onto Canada Place Way.

9 Waterfront Hotel
The public rooms of this waterfront hotel, at 999 Canada Place Way, house a rich diversity of watercolours, oil paintings and prints. In the lobby, a 3-m (10-foot) high vellum map celebrates the third (1790) and final voyage of Captain Cook to Vancouver. Elsewhere flamboyant abstracts, bright still lifes and glorious landscapes share wall space with antique saris, Northwest native art, antique maps and etchings.
Walk back along Canada Place Way to Burrard St, then south to just beyond Hastings St.

10 The Marine Building
Across Burrard Street stands the Marine Building, which was constructed on the eve of the Great Depression. Intricate art inside and out emphasises marine transportation. Terracotta insets on the façade depict trains, planes and zeppelins. Brass strippings of seahorses and octopuses frame the doors. Lobby walls in sea-green and gold feature ship prows jutting out, waves billowing beneath and full sails above. Light filters through a stained-glass fanlight to illuminate a marble mosaic on the floor.
Continue down Burrard St back to the start of the walk.

Nearby
Holy Rosary, Cathedral

Gardens and parks

Every February, when most of Canada is still covered in ice and snow, the first crocuses of spring poke their heads above ground to take a look at Vancouver and Victoria. The temperate coastal climate, ample sunshine and abundant rainfall encourage and ensure a great diversity of colourful flora. The greenery, which reigns supreme most of the year, is upstaged by riots of colourful blossom in spring and summer.

Nature has been kind to Vancouver

There are more than 150 gardens and parks in Vancouver, not counting the hundreds of thousands of private yards and gardens. Two of the prettiest public oases in the city differ greatly in character. Wild and rambling Stanley Park (*see pp70–73*) is Western, while the Dr Sun Yat-Sen Chinese Garden (*see p30*) is typically Eastern.

Botanical Gardens at the University of British Columbia

This showcase of plants from around the world includes a physic garden for medicinal herbs, planted around a sundial in the geometric design of a 16th-century herb garden. Horticulturists here have developed such new plants as the Emerald Carpet, a practical, low-spreading ground-cover plant with little flowers. The Arbour Garden provides cool shade where vines abound year round, while the Food Garden grows fruit trees trained in traditional styles, and the latest vegetables. The Asian Garden features 300 species of rhododendrons, along with kiwi fruit vines and magnolias.
6804 Southwest Marine Drive. Tel: (604)
822 4208; www.ubcbotanicalgarden.org.
Open: daily 10am–6pm (2.30pm in winter). Admission charge (free in winter).

Nitobe Memorial Garden

Reflecting the private retreats of Japan, gentle walkways meander through artistically pruned cherry, maple and pine trees, and layouts of sand and rock, to a tiny teahouse. The cherry blossoms in April or May and the iris blooms in late June are spectacular.
Across the street from the UBC Botanical Gardens. Tel: (604) 822 6038;
www.nitobe.org. Open: daily 10am–6pm (2.30pm in winter). Admission charge (free in winter).

Park and Tilford Gardens

This privately owned hideaway offers a delightful variety of plantings and landscape themes.
333 Brooksbank Ave, North Vancouver. Tel: (604) 984 8200. Open: daily 9am–sunset. Free admission.

Queen Elizabeth Park

This 52-hectare (128-acre) former stone quarry, transformed into sunken gardens, is a favourite site for bridal couples and wedding photos amid lawns, trees, shrubs and flowers. It is the highest spot in the city (152m/499 feet), so views are spectacular. The blossoms are at their best in late May and June, when azaleas and rhododendrons create a brilliant kaleidoscope of colour. An arboretum on the east side showcases trees and shrubs indigenous to the BC coast.

There is also a rose garden, a pitch-and-putt golf course (*tel: (604) 874 8336*), 20 tennis courts, and a restaurant looking out to the city. The Bloedel Floral Conservatory (*tel: (604) 257 8584*), a 20-m (66-foot) high triodetic dome consisting of 1,490 plexiglas bubbles, houses a tropical garden with more than 100 colourful birds flying free, and an arid area with cacti, and seasonal floral displays.
33rd Ave at Cambie St. Tel: (604) 257 8570; www.city.vancouver.bc.ca/parks/ parks/queenelizabeth/. Open: daily 9am–8pm in summer; Oct–mid-Apr 10am–5pm. Admission charge to the conservatory.

VanDusen Botanical Garden

This spectacular 22-hectare (55-acre) garden in the heart of Vancouver has matured into a botanical garden of international stature since opening to the public in 1975. The mild Vancouver climate allows the cultivation of an outstanding plant collection which is a delight at any time of the year. There are over 7,500 different kinds of plants assembled from six continents. Specific garden areas are planted to illustrate botanical relationships, such as the Rhododendron Walk, or geographical origins as in the Sino Himalayan Garden. These areas are set amid rolling lawns, tranquil lakes and dramatic rock-work, with vistas of the mountains and the Vancouver cityscape.
5251 Oak St, not far from Queen Elizabeth Park. Tel: (604) 878 9274; www.vandusengarden.org. Open: daily 10am–dusk. Admission charge.

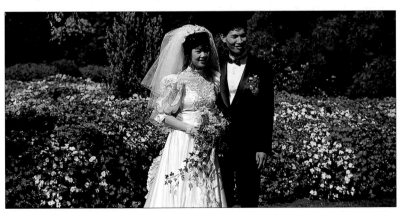

Vancouver's many parks are loved for wedding shots

Walk: Pacific Spirit Park

A walk in the wild woods on the edge of the city offers patches of ocean framed by red cedars where squirrels scuffle through the underbrush, birds sing and serenity is all around – just a few of the pleasures of Pacific Spirit Park. Personnel working on the trails are also helpful.
Allow about 2 hours, plus time for birdwatching.

Begin at Chancellor Blvd, where the extra lane for parking begins, just beyond the Pacific Spirit Park sign. Start on the Pioneer Trail, then follow the first right to the Spanish Trail, which meanders through the woods to Spanish Banks Beach or loops back on to the Pioneer Trail to the entrance.

The **Pioneer Trail** and **Spanish Trail** loop, which is about 2km (1¼ miles) long, can be muddy in sections, but this is to be expected in a rainforest. The Spanish Trail heads north into tall trees and undergrowth, and for a while parallels the south edge of a tree-choked ravine. A few metres off the trail, walkers can peer down into its leafy depths.

Just a few minutes into this forest, traffic sounds fade, sunlight filters through branches overhead, and the aroma of earth and cedar fills the air. Lush ferns, salal, holly and salmonberry bushes line the trails. Spiders' webs glisten and mushrooms cluster on fallen trunks. An occasional woodpecker drums on rotting trees, and tiny wrens and juncos flit about. A chipmunk scurries down a Douglas fir and sometimes frogs serenade. Although raccoons, weasels, skunks, otters and foxes make their homes in the undergrowth, they are usually shy when people are around.

Where the trail slopes down sharply and becomes rougher, it soon divides. The Spanish Trail heads steeply downhill and north to Spanish Banks Beach, soon visible through the trees. The Pioneer Trail turns west, through a wooden gate.

Climb over a fallen tree trunk to an open glade called the Plains of Abraham. At the turn of the 20th century, a John Stewart ran a dairy farm here, but the once-visible foundations have now become overgrown with fireweed and blackberry bushes. A sign to the southwest indicates the Pioneer Trail, the corduroy road built by Stewart so that he could haul his milk to market.

For a longer walk, cross the western edge of the clearing and follow the winding trail north to the cliff edge, where it swings west to parallel the clifftops and provides views of Burrard Inlet and the North Shore Mountains.

The trail eventually ends at a clearing on North West Marine Drive across from the beach. Any blue herons flying overhead are probably returning to their homes hidden in these woods.

Some 34 trails meander 53km (33 miles) through Pacific Spirit Park, several beginning from the park information office. All that is needed is a map and a reasonable sense of direction. Many are popular with dog walkers, horse riders, joggers, hikers and mountain bikers. Film makers occasionally adapt the park for sets, varying from the Amazon jungle to rural Pennsylvania.

The park is about a 20-minute drive from downtown; count on half an hour by bus (No 25). Maps are available at the park information office on W 16th Ave and at information boards at many trailheads (contact GVRD Parks at tel: (604) 224 5739).

Rainforest at Pacific Spirit Park

Walk: Granville Island

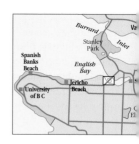

Granville Island is actually a peninsula. Once a swampy, tidal flat and later the industrial heart of Vancouver, these 15 hectares (37 acres) of land are now an urban oasis of parks, walkways and renovated warehouses, popular for the many shops and galleries, restaurants and other diversions located here. (*See www.granvilleisland.com*)
Allow about 2 hours, plus extra time for more leisurely browsing and a meal.

Walk south from downtown for 10 minutes to the foot of Hornby St or the Aquatic Centre and take the five-minute Aquabus mini-ferry ride across False Creek. There is complimentary three-hour parking for both cars and boats on the island, but places are extremely hard to find. It is much better to go on foot.

1 Arts Club theatres

Overlooking the ferry terminal are two Arts Club theatres. Walk right between them to the Information Centre which offers an audio-visual presentation on the evolution of the area.

Northwest is the Public Market, well worth a stroll through, if only to enjoy the aroma of a great array of local and imported fruits and vegetables, fish and seafood, plants and flowers, and fast-food stands. On the waterfront, a bevy of buskers, including colourful clowns and jugglers, and sometimes mediocre musicians, entertain benches of visitors munching Vietnamese salad rolls and Italian lasagne.

Northwest of the market is a good place to watch the yachts and motor-boats slip out to English Bay beyond. The deck at Bridges Restaurant (there may be a queue) is a super spot to sit in the sun or watch the sunset.
Turn south into Duranleau St.

2 Duranleau Street

Duranleau Street sports a series of maritime shops selling rugged outdoor wear, scuba gear, yacht fittings and other nautical equipment and wares. Across the street, the Net Loft shelters a dozen shops, including Edie's Hats with a selection of stylish headgear; The Postcard Place; Paper Ya's which features handmade writing paper and other paper art from around the world; Mesa, where a weaver may be at work at the loom; and the Wickaninnish Gallery of native jewellery and sculptures.
Cross Anderson St.

3 Granville Island Brewery

Across Anderson Street, the brewery produces a popular preservative-free light lager (Bavarian-style Pilsner), and offers free tastings every afternoon.
Cross over to Cartwright St.

4 Cartwright Street

The Kids Only Market houses two dozen shops and activity areas, and a playcare centre for pre-schoolers. Just beyond the Waterfront Theatre is the supervised summertime Water Park, where children douse each other with revolving water cannons, while parents watch over a coffee or lunch at adjacent Cat's Meow restaurant which has a children's play area inside for rainy days. The rest of Cartwright Street is lined with art studios, galleries and craft shops, and leads east to the Granville Island Hotel.

Continue east to the Granville Island Hotel and the Sea Village.

5 Sea Village

On the north shore, near a big, rusting crane overhead, is a fleet of floating homes, many with skylights and patios crowded with plants and flowers. The Sea Village is a private residential complex, but walk part way down the ramp to see a colourful collection of rural mailboxes.

Continue along the boardwalk northwest to the Emily Carr Institute of Art & Design.

6 Emily Carr Institute of Art & Design

Here, big windows reveal students at work. Visitors are welcome to view the student art exhibits in the foyer. Next door is the Ocean Cement factory, which somehow seems to belong and makes the area more interesting. Beyond a few more craft shops along the shore is the ferry dock.

Active visitors can sign up for classes at the art studios, enjoy a reading from West Coast Psychics above the Arts Club Lounge, or go parasailing over English Bay. The more adventurous can rent a one- or two-seater kayak to paddle up False Creek, past the floating homes to the Science Centre.

Return to the ferry.

Nearby
Aquatic Centre, Waterfront Theatre

Vancouver Harbour

Vancouver Harbour is Canada's largest port and one of the top 20 in the world – the country's gateway to the Pacific Rim – and it plays a key role in international trade. Every year more than 3,000 ships, most flying foreign flags, carry bulk, general and containerised cargo between Vancouver and a hundred other ports around the world. The two dozen terminals circling Vancouver Harbour move more than 70 million tonnes of cargo annually. Enterprises engaged in this trade range from BC Sugar and United Grain Growers to Cassier Mining. For more information visit *www.portvancouver.com*

The busy harbour at False Creek

Beyond the Inner Harbour east of Second Narrows Bridge are several oil refineries and a major sulphur export operation at Port Moody. About 35km south of downtown, near the BC Ferries dock at Tsawwassen, the Westshore Terminals at Roberts Bank ship coal, sulphur and lumber to other countries.

Canada Place Promenade

Canada Place has a wrap-around public promenade for observing the Inner Harbour. A self-directed walk, called 'Promenade into History', follows a series of plaques describing historical waterfront events. The promenade also provides great dockside viewing of some of the world's most luxurious cruise ships, which run from here to Alaska from May to September. Canada Place is home to the CNIMAX Theatre.
Tel: (604) 682 IMAX;
www.imax.com/vancouver

Panoramic vantage points

Harbour-view rooms at the Pan Pacific, Waterfront Centre and Renaissance hotels enable visitors to Vancouver to get orientated quickly. Much cheaper are the bird's-eye vantage points at Vistas, the revolving restaurant atop the Renaissance Hotel, where visitors can enjoy regional specialities or coffee and dessert as the harbour panorama moves by.

The Lookout!, a circular observation deck high above Harbour Centre (*tel: (604) 689 0421*), also affords a 360-degree view of the harbour and the city, and photographic plaques and decorative display panels relate the history and character of the area. But there is an admission charge.

Views from the water

For a view of the harbour from the water, take the SeaBus (*tel: (604) 953 3333*) from the downtown terminal to North Vancouver. Alternatively, contact any Travel InfoCentre (*tel: (604) 683 2000; www.tourismvancouver.com*) for details about harbour cruises.

Waterfront parks

Several parks around Burrard Inlet offer great picnic spots and harbour views. From the Stanley Park Port Look Out, on the seawall just south of Brockton Point, almost the whole harbour is visible, and a series of plaques outlines port operations.

Much smaller **Portside Park**, just east of Canada Place at the foot of Main Street, offers grassy slopes, children's play areas and a good view of various marine activities. **New Brighton Park**, further east and adjacent to the Alberta Wheat Pool just off McGill Street, has a pool (*tel: (604) 298 0222*), a pier, lots of open space, views of grain and forest products handling facilities and the ships sailing through the Second Narrows.

Waterfront Park, located between the Lonsdale Quay and the Pacific Marine Training Institute in North Vancouver, provides a panorama of the harbour and the city skyline. Harbour View Park, located further east on a narrow strip of land at the mouth of Lynn Creek, features a creek-side walking trail and a platform for observing the loading and unloading of forest products.

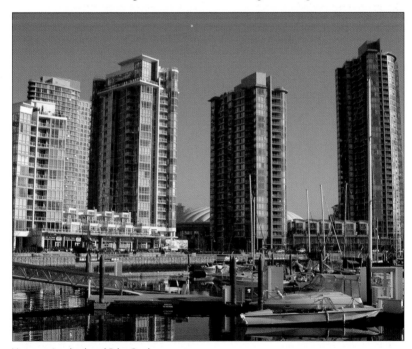

Vancouver's redeveloped False Creek

Vancouver is the largest port in Canada, providing the vital link with the Pacific Rim nations. It will come as no surprise, therefore, to discover that Vancouver Harbour was once almost exclusively industrial. However, this is no longer the case. Extensive development is underway, concentrated in three main areas, all of which are on the waterfront: Coal Harbour near Stanley Park; Yaletown where redevelopment is complete; and East False Creek near the Science Centre.

The development at Coal Harbour is one of the most extensive waterfront revitalisations in North America. Stretching east of Stanley Park to the Trade and Convention Centre at the foot of Burrard Street, the city's newest community comprises a marina, park, community centre, offices and retail development. A number of townhouses and residential towers offer upmarket living, a short 10-minute walk from downtown Vancouver. When complete, the development is expected to cater to approximately 3,500 people.

In the 1980s Yaletown was the industrial backyard of downtown Vancouver, full of warehouses and light industry – it even had a sawmill. Today, while the distinctive stone-paved streets and many stone and brick buildings still remain, the warehouses have been replaced by trendy furniture showrooms and design studios. The streets are dotted with restaurants, nightclubs and coffee houses. Residential development in this now up-scale and popular area hugs the waterfront. The redevelopment along East False Creek – a cluster of towers offering some 1,000 residential units and 16,250sq m (175,000 square feet) of commercial space – completes the revitalisation of this erstwhile neglected harbour area.

The pace of life in that part of the harbour occupied by pleasure craft is gentle. Residents here usually find time to chat and are friendly to visitors. One resident, who has worked here aboard his floating electronic cottage/houseboat for 20 years, says the tides are for him the pulse of Mother Nature. If he were never to leave his home for a whole year, he would still travel over 5km (3 miles), since harbour tides advance and retreat as much as 4.5m (15 feet) twice daily.

A floating house off Granville Island

Canada geese paddle up to his houseboat most mornings for breakfast, while hunched blue herons stalk along the shore for snacks, and kingfishers dive for minnows. Loons and cormorants patrol the waters, along with ever-present shrieking seagulls.

Starfish and mussels hug the pillars that keep the docks in place, while crabs crawl and feed along the bottom. Harbour seals occasionally watch from further offshore.

In winter, harbour dwellers can pull out binoculars and look up to Grouse Mountain across Burrard Inlet to see if there's still room for more skiers on the slopes. It's quite a lifestyle!

Tour: boat ride on a bus

The SeaBus provides an inexpensive harbour cruise, along with a great opportunity to explore Lonsdale Quay and Waterfront Park in North Vancouver. The crossing takes 15 minutes.

Allow 2 hours.

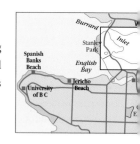

Start the tour at the Waterfront Station, located at the end of Water St.

1 SeaBus terminal

Tall, creamy pillars mark the entrance to this classic old brick building. The beautifully renovated interior of the terminal showcases a series of paintings from 1916 of the Rocky Mountains, looking down on a large lobby surrounded by several shops, fast-food stops and coffee bars.

Pause briefly on the overhead ramp en route to the SeaBus to watch railcars being shunted ahead and back over the shining rails, as trains load and unload. Then board the SeaBus for the sail across the inner harbour.

The SeaBuses, appropriately named the SS *Beaver* and the SS *Otter*, have no outside decks, but the windows provide a maritime pastiche of freighters with many foreign flags, luxury cruise ships sailing to and from Alaska, a variety of smaller pleasure craft, and float planes taking off and landing. North looms the imposing majesty of the Coast Range, west the forest green peninsula of Stanley Park, and the Lions Gate Bridge. Southward stand the shining sails of Canada Place and the mirrored high-rises of downtown, in sharp contrast to an eastward-stretching line of old buildings huddled along the waterfront.

The SeaBus ferry offers great views across Burrard Inlet

After disembarking on the North Shore, turn right to Lonsdale Quay.

2 Lonsdale Quay

The ground floor of this airy glass and steel structure, right at the water's edge, features a public market with a colourful assortment of local and imported fruit and vegetables, meat and fish, breads and pastries, cut and dried flowers and potted plants. Inexpensive fast-food restaurants serve everything from Italian pizza to Vietnamese salad rolls. A snack, a coffee or a cold drink on the outside deck includes the stunning harbour view. The second level has a charming collection of gift shops and boutiques, while the third level is the entrance to the Lonsdale Quay Hotel.

West from the Quay and the SeaBus Terminal lies Waterfront Park.

3 Waterfront Park

A leisurely stroll along the meandering, wide, paved walkway takes about half an hour. Along the seawall, signs identify prominent downtown buildings. A short wooden pier with a covered (it does rain here occasionally!) observation deck and benches juts out over the water. During the summer

months, musical concerts are held here on many Sunday afternoons and, at other times, local clubs enjoy kite-flying, square dancing, vintage car shows and native pow-wows. A noticeboard at the west end of the park lists events, dates and times.

Beside the walkway stands a huge series of irregular, separate steel arches spanning a shrub-covered gully, a modernistic sculpture entitled *Cathedral* by artist Douglas Senft. A little further west, an elegant, stylised sundial dominates Sailor's Point Plaza. The base of the sculpture contains tiny sketches of sunken ships. The plaza is dedicated to people who have lost their lives at sea in both peace and wartime. A plaque on the plaza celebrates Captain George Vancouver, the European who discovered and named Burrard Inlet.

Before heading back, peek through the windows of the Pacific Marine Training Institute to see the assembly of nautical devices used by modern mariners in training.

The SeaBus runs every 15 to 30 minutes from 6am to 6pm and at half-hour intervals during the evening.
Tel: (604) 953 3333; www.translink.bc.ca

The Mansion

Historic houses

Vancouver, like Los Angeles, seems to have suffered from the philosophy of down with the old and up with the new, as far as preserving historic ('heritage') homes is concerned. But a few treasures remain.

The Mansion

This elegant Victorian stone mansion was built in 1900 by American sugar tycoon BT Rogers as a family residence. The original home had 18 fireplaces with self-cleaning flues (several of which remain), and a pantry cooled by ice. The walls are oak-panelled, and the floors laid with teak from Fiji. A spectacular stained-glass window overlooks the staircase which rises from the main foyer. It depicts three women believed to represent the virtues of faith, hope and charity, and the graces of wisdom, youth and beauty. The background is decked with BC wild flowers and seashells.

Other features of the house include a walk-in humidor for cigar smokers and, outside, a wrought-iron fence built from balconies of the old San Francisco City Hall. It now houses an Italian restaurant called Romano's Macaroni Grill, noted for its good pasta, which is open for both lunch and dinner.
1523 Davie St, a five-minute walk from English Bay. Tel: (604) 689 4334.

Irving House

'The handsomest, the best and most home-like house of which BC can yet boast' was the 1865 newspaper description of this 14-room home, which originally belonged to 'King of the River' Captain William Irving. The small parlour and master bedroom contain Irving's furniture, including a red rocking chair from a Fraser River sternwheeler, a piano shipped round Cape Horn in 1858 and a black horsehair settee transported across the plains from Missouri. The kitchen features a classic black and chrome pioneer stove laden with cast-iron pots and flat irons, and a hand-pumped vacuum cleaner. The kitchen floor was laid and caulked like the deck of a ship. The nursery upstairs contains a collection of dolls from the 19th century. In the library are a roll-top desk, a smoking table, a pump organ, a 17th-century grandfather clock and some fine Indian baskets.
302 Royal Ave, New Westminster. Tel: (604) 527 4640. Open: May–mid-Sept, Wed–Sun 12.30–4.30pm. Admission by donation.

Roedde House

Built in 1893 by the German immigrant Gustav Roedde, Vancouver's first bookbinder, this house is part of a park site that includes nine Victorian West End houses, most of them renovated for family accommodation.

Designed by FM Rattenbury, the architect responsible for the Empress

Hotel, Roedde House is built in simple Queen Anne style, with a cupola, bay windows, an upstairs porch and a downstairs veranda. The interior has been furnished with period furniture to reflect city life at the turn of the 20th century. *1415 Barclay St, a 10-minute walk from the city centre. Tel: (604) 684 7040; www.roeddehouse.org. Guided tours on Wed–Fri 2–4pm, Sun 2–4pm; group tours by appointment. Admission charge.*

Le Gavroche

A good way to make the past present is by enjoying a meal in a heritage home restaurant. Named after the street urchin in *Les Misérables*, Le Gavroche was established in 1979 in a refurbished three-storey Victorian house whose roof is green with moss, looking out to the Bayshore Hotel and Coal Harbour. The intimate, dimly-lit interior, with its oak floors, flickering flames in the wood-burning fireplace, and dark floral-print wallpaper contrasting with white tablecloths, quickly transports diners back to a more romantic time. The restaurant is renowned for refined service, fine French cuisine and one of the city's best wine collections. *1616 Alberni St. Tel: (604) 685 3924; www.legavroche.com*

The Victorian façade of Roedde House

Detail of carving on a
Haida pole

Museums

A wide variety of city museums provides an in-depth look
at the history and cultural life of Vancouver and BC, with
exhibits ranging from food and maritime history to sports
and First Nations cultures.

Museum of Anthropology
The Museum of Anthropology at the
University of British Columbia,
probably Canada's most memorable
museum, is best known for its superb
collection of art and artefacts of the
province's First Nations peoples. The
spectacular concrete-and-glass structure
sits on a cliff overlooking English Bay
and, beyond, the North Shore
Mountains and Howe Sound. Inside the
MOA, as it is affectionately called, a
dozen galleries house a great variety of
objects, which express the complex
social and ceremonial life of many
cultures from around the world.

Entrance to the World of Art
The museum's cedar entrance doors,
designed and carved by contemporary
Ksan master carvers, depict the joining
of heaven and earth in the creation of
the first Gitksan people. The doors,
along with the adjoining side panels,
form a rectangular structure inspired by
the traditional Indian bent box.
Carvings from traditional West Coast
house interiors, with illustrations
showing their original placement,
border the entrance ramp. At the base of
the ramp, a bear sculpted by the
contemporary artist Bill Reid, of the
Haida people, is one of the few

touchable exhibits in the museum. Be
sure to feel its square snout and large
teeth, nostrils and ears, characteristic of
Haida bear carvings.

The spectacular Great Hall
In the Great Hall, natural light streams
through 14-m (46-foot) high windows,
which illuminate an exquisite assembly
of weathered cedar totem poles. Totem
poles do not usually tell a story, but
depict creatures representing the
genealogy of the families that raised
them. Ravens, bears, beavers, frogs,
eagles and wolves are often an integral
part of tribal crests. Totem poles have
traditionally been raised to identify
families or to commemorate the
departed, and a raising continues to
be an occasion for a *potlatch*, or
celebration. A selection of red cedar
chests, carved canoes and dishes
complements the display.

Highlights of the galleries
The Masterpiece Gallery houses an
intriguing collection of intricately
carved miniatures in silver, gold,
argillite, ivory, bone, horn and wood,
mostly dating from the 19th century.
   But the highlight of the contemporary
collection is the acclaimed sculpture *The
Raven and The First Men*, carved in

laminated yellow cedar by Bill Reid, and displayed in a skylighted rotunda. The sculpture is a dramatic portrayal of the birth of mankind, with the first Haida people emerging both frontwards and backwards from a partially open clam shell.

Behind this sculpture, several cases display 30 of Reid's smaller carvings in cedar, boxwood and argillite, along with some gold and silver jewellery pieces. These works span 40 years of creative activity, from early explorations in Haida design to his distinctive, mature style, now recognised around the world.

The Research Collections, since the museum is both a public and a teaching institution, feature a visible storage system, with a series of glass-covered drawers and cases that let visitors see but not touch more than 10,000 objects, arranged in cultural and artefact categories.

The outdoor exhibits
One of the best exhibits is outdoors on the grassy area between the museum and the cliff. The Kwakiutl, Haida and Gitksan totem poles standing here with two Haida houses, one for the living and one for the dead, are completely at one with nature.

On the UBC campus at 6393 Northwest Marine Drive. Tel: (604) 822 3825; www.moa.ubc.ca. Open: daily, summer 10am–5pm (9pm on Tue); winter, Wed–Sun 11am–5pm (9pm on Tue). Closed: Mon. Admission charge, except Tue evenings.

The Museum of Anthropology displays a fine collection of Northwest Coast Indian art

BC Golf Museum

A collection of golf memorabilia to delight the enthusiastic golfer.
2545 Blanca St.
Tel: (604) 222 4653;
www.bcgolfmuseum.org.
Open: Tue–Sun noon–4pm.

BC Sports Hall of Fame and Museum

This museum provides high-tech, hands-on sports entertainment. Visitors can run, throw, climb and row their way through the computer-enhanced Hall of Champions which honours BC's elite athletes and teams, or test their athletic skills against top competitors in the Participation Gallery. The museum covers 150 years of history, from 1850s Native games to videos of recent sporting events.
At BC Place Stadium.
Tel: (604) 687 5520;
www.bcplacestadium.com.
Open: daily 10am–5pm.
Admission charge.

Canadian Museum of Flight

This outdoor assembly of vintage aircraft includes bombers, biplanes, jets and helicopters. The museum also has a picnic area and playground for children.
Hanger 3, 5333-216 St,

Langley. Tel: (604) 532 0035;
www.canadianflight.org.
Open: daily 10am–4pm.
Admission charge.

Granville Island Model Trains Museum

Kids and train fanatics alike enjoy the huge collection of model and toy trains – said to be the world's largest such collection on display.
1502 Duranleau St.
Tel: (604) 483 1939;
www.modeltrainsmuseum.ca.
Open: Tue–Sun 10am–5.30pm. Admission charge.

HR MacMillan Space Centre

Multimedia astronomy shows, including special shows for children, and Canada's best laser light show, beamed on to a 20-m (66-foot) dome, bring the cosmos within reach. The cosmic Courtyard interactive gallery puts visitors at the controls. There is also a variety of special presentations in the GroundStation Canada mission control theatre, and exciting simulated journeys through space. The centre also has some authentic space artefacts to see and a real moon rock to touch.
1100 Chestnut St, Vanier

CAPTAIN GEORGE VANCOUVER

George Vancouver, an English youth of Dutch descent, joined the British navy at the age of 13, and went on to serve Captain Cook on his second and third voyages. In 1791, Captain Vancouver set out from England aboard HMS *Discovery*, sailed south around the Cape of Good Hope, and a year later reached the northern Pacific coast of North America. He had been tasked to survey the coast and negotiate a land settlement with Spanish Captain Bodega y Quadra, at Nootka, on what is now known as Vancouver Island.

Without realising that the Spaniards had charted this region before him, Vancouver claimed all the land he saw for King George III.

Vancouver returned to England in 1795 and died three years later aged 40. Spain, after the Mexican revolution, eventually abandoned all claims to the Pacific Northwest.

Park. Tel: (604) 738-STAR (7827);
www.hrmacmillanspacecentre.com.
Open: Tue–Sun 10am–5pm, and holidays;
(daily in July & Aug). Admission charge.

Vancouver Maritime Museum

This museum explores the maritime
world, with exciting tales of the sea and
hands-on activities in its Children's
Maritime Discovery Centre. There is a
huge collection of model ships and
many special exhibitions. The museum
is home to the *St Roch*, a two-masted
schooner which is now a National
Historic Site. Built in the 1920s, it
became the first ship to navigate
through the treacherous waters of the
Northwest Passage.

1905 Ogden Ave. Tel: (604) 257 8300;
www.vmm.bc.ca. Open: mid-May–mid-
Sept, Tue–Sun 10am–5pm; mid-
Sept–mid-May, Tue–Sat 10am–5pm,
Sun noon–5pm.
Closed: Mon & Christmas Day.
Tours available. Admission charge.

Vancouver Museum

This museum, which houses one of the
largest civic collections in Canada, is
devoted to regional history and the
First Nations, but also features
exhibitions of decorative arts from all
over the world.
1100 Chestnut St. Tel: (604) 736 4431.
Open: daily 10am–5pm; Thur 10am–9pm.
Closed Mon Sept–June. Admission charge.

Crab sculpture at the HR MacMillan Space Centre

On the totem trail

At least 8,000 years ago, Asian peoples who lived by hunting and gathering berries crossed the icy land bridge that is now the Bering Strait and drifted south along the Pacific coast of North America and into the interior. When the Europeans arrived in the late 18th century, an estimated 80,000 of these native 'Indians' were living in what is now known as BC. Within a century, however, two-thirds of them had died from imported diseases.

Today, there are once again about 80,000 people of native Indian ancestry living in BC. The Salish inhabit the southwest of the province (the Lower Mainland) and the southeastern part of Vancouver Island. On the west coast of Vancouver Island are the Nootka. Further north along the coast reside the Kwakiutl, Bella Coola, Tsimshian, Haida and Tlingit peoples. Almost 80 per cent of BC's land area is subject to 22 native land claims, including most of greater Vancouver. The struggle to regain self-esteem and self-reliance has been accelerating. There has been a visible renaissance in the arts, in totem poles, masks, talking sticks, bent boxes, canoes, clothing and jewellery.

Totem poles, the largest wood-carvings known, are scattered throughout Vancouver. Some of the best are in Stanley Park, at the Museum of Anthropology and at the Capilano Suspension Bridge (*www.capbridge.com*).

Carving of totem poles can be viewed at The Big House at Capilano Suspension Bridge. Some of these carved cedar poles are memorials to the dead, others portray family trees, while still others relate mythological adventures.

Carved in a stylised realism, totem poles are sometimes difficult to decipher, but here are some of the creatures commonly seen. The thunderbird is the creator and controller of all elements and spirits. The raven is credited with providing light, fire and water. The whale symbolises strength and bravery. The bear, regarded as an elder kinsman, represents strength, authority and mobility. The eagle represents wisdom, authority and power, and the salmon abundance and prosperity.

The exquisite artistry of the Northwest Coast Indian totem poles in Vancouver's Stanley Park

The Orpheum: a Canadian classic

Here in one of North America's youngest cities, the patina of the past so prevalent in Europe is most wonderfully preserved in the Orpheum theatre. This gracious old building boasts a history of hosting such great artists as Charlie Chaplin, Igor Stravinsky and Helen Hayes. Its grand opening in 1927 was a social highlight in city history. The Orpheum, with 2,800 seats, was then the largest theatre on the Pacific coast. The premiere featured a silent movie, but people really came to see the vaudeville: Marie White and the Blue Slickers, dance exponents Chaney and Fox, Ethel Davis in refreshing song chatter, and everybody's favourite, Toto the clown with his little dog, Whiskey.

Interior and backstage wonders

The Orpheum has always been a star, even with mediocre performers. Originally built as a link in the Chicago-based theatre chain, it was designed in conservative Spanish Renaissance style, with a basic colour scheme of antique ivory and gold. Ornamented pilasters and colonnades, highlighted with imitation and sometimes real gold leaf, contrasted with rich tapestries of black and gold arabesques, creating an aura of exotic luxury. Dramatic maroon velvet draperies lent a regal touch. A hundred glittering chandeliers lighted the hall.

Beneath the stage, an electrically operated elevator raised and lowered three big Wurlitzer organs, which sounded like a full orchestra. One is still played a few times every year. An animal room accommodated the assortment of dogs, monkeys, tigers and elephants featured in some of the shows. An efficient ventilation system changed the air in the theatre every three minutes. One Orpheum manager said the downstairs was spooky and uncomfortably reminiscent of *The Phantom of the Opera*.

Famous Players and the talkies

During the early 1930s, when live music faded and talking pictures took over, the Orpheum passed into the hands of Famous Players Theatres. The Nabob Company sponsored elegant afternoon teas on the mezzanine.

One of the Orpheum's proudest moments was probably the Canadian premiere of *Gone With The Wind* in 1939. The theatre has attracted countless famous faces, including Marilyn Monroe, who came in 1956 to publicise *Gentlemen Prefer Blondes*.

Snack-vending machines appeared in the Orpheum in 1942, and a confectionery counter in 1945. By 1950, usherettes were selling confections from trays in the auditorium. From 1943 to 1954, Nabob's Harmony House was broadcast from coast to coast from 'Canada's most beautiful theatre'. One of the last *grandes premieres* was *King Rat* in 1965, with a guest appearance by author James Clavell, then living in West Vancouver.

Meanwhile, the Vancouver Symphony

Orchestra had been a frequent performer from the early 1930s.

Restoration to former glory

In 1973, Famous Players announced that the Orpheum would be gutted to create six mini-cinemas, reflecting a continuing trend towards smaller theatres. Vancouverites wrote 8,500 letters in protest. Consequently, the city purchased the Orpheum for $3.9 million, and spent almost as much restoring the acoustics and fine furnishings. Octogenarian artist and decorator Tony Heinsbergen, who had worked on the original structure in 1927, supervised the interior decoration and painted the mural on the massive 20-m (66-foot) dome. Florentine Joseph Tinucci did much of the ornate and decorative plasterwork, and reproduced the columns that are now part of the soundshell.

In 1977, the Orpheum reopened, once again a breathtaking beauty and the finest heritage concert hall in the country. In 1983, a new foyer was completed, and the Orpheum was declared a National Historic Site. Today, the Orpheum is home to the Vancouver Symphony Orchestra and the BC Entertainment Hall of Fame.
884 Granville, Smythe St at Seymour. Tel: (604) 665 3050; www.city.vancouver.bc.ca/theatres. Tours on request (charge).

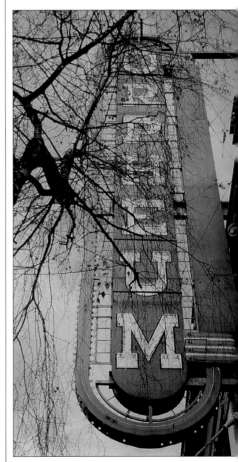

One of the city's major landmarks

Vancouver Symphony Orchestra

The historic Orpheum Theatre has been home to the Vancouver Symphony Orchestra since 1930. Each year, apart from a full concert season extending from October to April, the orchestra presents special outdoor concerts around the region in summer. In September 2000, Bramwell Tovey became Music Director. Also gifted as an orator, Tovey gives regular lectures on forthcoming programmes an hour before the performance starts – arrive an hour early in order to avail yourself of this opportunity.
*601 Smythe St. Tel: (604) 876 3434; www.vancouversymphony.ca.
Concert tickets are available online at www.ticketmaster.ca*

Places of worship

There are dozens of places of worship in Vancouver, thanks to the variety of visitors from all over the world who have settled here. The following are a few that might be of interest to anyone, regardless of creed. A listing of churches is found in the Practical Guide section on page 184.

St Andrew's-Westley Church on Burrard St

Buddhist Temple

This temple is an exquisite example of Chinese palatial architecture, with gilded porcelain tiles and flying rooftop dragons. The interior is an artistic showcase of oriental sculpture, painting, carpentry and embroidery. An outdoor courtyard encloses a beautiful collection of bonsai plants and a ceramic mural of Kuan-Yin-Bodhisattva.

A 30-minute drive south from downtown; turn west at the exit by Fantasy Gardens towards Steveston. 9160 Steveston Highway, Richmond. Tel: (604) 274 2822. Open: daily 10am–5pm. Free admission.

Canadian Memorial Church

Shortly after World War I, Chaplain George Fallis came to Vancouver with the idea of building a memorial to Canadians who had served in the war. He found a congregation with the same idea, solicited the support of local leaders, and then headed east across Canada to find further funding. The result was the Canadian Memorial Church, which opened in 1928 at the 11th hour of the 11th day of the 11th month – mortgage-free.

The church is constructed in greystone Gothic-style. The main attraction is the stained-glass windows, each of which depicts a biblical scene. The provincial coats of arms beneath are flanked by historical illustrations.

The BC window depicts a soldier's faith, with Christ meeting a Roman centurion pleading on behalf of his palsied servant. The historic panels show Captain Vancouver at Nootka Sound in 1792 and Simon Fraser exploring the Fraser River in 1808.

The Nova Scotia window illustrates the arrival of Jacques Cartier in 1543 and of Lord Rollo, the first Englishman, in 1759. The Yukon window depicts the Chilkoot Pass in 1898 and a Royal Mail dog team with carriole.

The spectacular chancel window portrays a biblical motif of sacrifice and young manhood. The all-Canada window facing north depicts the services rendered by all men and women of Canada throughout World War I.

The windows are interesting for their comments on world peace and history and for their exquisite craftsmanship.
At the southwest corner of Burrard St & 15th Ave. Tel: (604) 731 3101; www.canadianmemorial.org.
Open: regular church services are held on Sun morning at 10.30am, but for many visitors who may prefer to study the windows in relative solitude, staff at the

community centre, adjacent to the church on 16th Ave, keep the keys and escort those interested to the chapel during regular business hours.

Christ Church Cathedral

Located in the heart of downtown Vancouver, this century-old sanctuary looks as though it should be nestled into a green valley in rural England. Of special interest are the English and Canadian stained-glass windows, and a tableau of the Crucifixion.
690 Burrard St. Tel: (604) 682 3848;
www.cathedral.vancouver.bc.ca.
Open: Mon–Fri 9.30am–4pm.
Free admission.

Westminster Abbey

This modern Benedictine monastery is both a high school and a degree-granting theological seminary. Every Sunday the ten bells of the 50m tower chime over the valley to announce Mass. Resident monks create and restore paintings and other forms of art in an atmosphere of peace and tranquillity. Various sculptures, stained-glass windows and murals decorate the monastery. Overnight rooms are available (reservations recommended), as St Benedict believed that there should always be guests at a monastery.
34224 Dewdney Trunk Rd, near the town of Mission, an hour's drive east from Vancouver. Tel: (604) 826 8975.
Open: Mon–Fri 1.30–4pm; Sun 2–4pm. Guided tours available. Modest dress requested. Donations accepted.

The beautiful Buddhist Temple in Richmond

Science World

A hundred years ago, the site of Science World was a swamp covered with water. Today, its silver geodesic sphere is a city landmark, shimmering over the eastern end of False Creek. Billed as the most curious place on earth, this science complex attracts 500,000 inquiring minds a year. Most visitors like to spend two to three hours at Science World, and many enjoy lunch or a snack before moving on. The street-level foyer houses the Information Centre, cloakrooms, telephones and an interesting gift shop.

The mysteries of science are entertainingly unravelled for visitors

Scientific wonders discovered

On the street level beyond the entrance are This Day In Science, which highlights current events, and the puzzling optical effects of the Visual Illusions exhibit.

In the Eureka! Gallery on the second level, visitors can learn about everything from potential energy to sound through bright, engaging exhibits and games. The nearby Search Gallery focuses on the natural history of BC. There are tree roots hanging from the ceiling, a crawl-through beaver lodge, a hollow tree and a see-through beehive.

Bodyworks offers interactive exhibits that investigate individual strength, endurance, speed, reaction time, dexterity, accuracy, memory and much more. The science behind human performance and the relationship between athletic and everyday activities are the focus of this new exhibition.

In the Feature Gallery, interactive exhibits which change regularly might include kaleidoscopes; challenging puzzles with tangrams (Chinese puzzles which consist of several basic shapes which can be combined to form a great variety of other figures) and geometric shapes; and the study of physiognomy, in which the curious can observe how faces express feeling, deceive, encode identity and record experiences.

Big-screen excitement

The third level houses the 400-seat OMNIMAX Theatre (the screen is 27m/89 feet wide), where the audience is surrounded with awesome images on one of the world's largest domed screens and engulfed in wrap-around sound. These larger-than-life shows may cover such subjects as the origin of the universe, life above and below the ocean, and the explosive ring of fire circling the Pacific Rim.

Dazzling demonstrations

Science World presents audience participation shows daily at Centre Stage. These lively and entertaining programmes focus on such diverse subjects as bubbles, balance, kinetic engineering and liquid nitrogen. Designed to keep youngsters in touch with discoveries in science and technology, and its expanding frontier, Science World organises special events for children from time to time.

1455 Quebec St, across from the Main St SkyTrain station. Tel: (604) 443 7443; www.scienceworld.bc.ca.
Open: Mon–Fri 10am–5pm, Sat–Sun 10am–6pm. Admission charge.

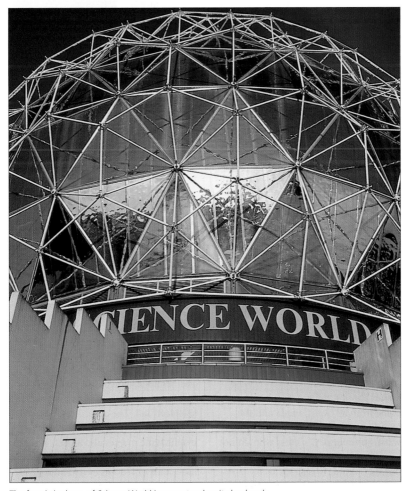

The futuristic dome of Science World is a spectacular city landmark

Stanley Park

In a province as vast and varied as BC, there are many close-to-nature hideaways. But it is relatively rare to find an urban wilderness so accessible to so many people as Stanley Park. About a 10-minute walk from downtown, the park covers an area of 400 hectares (988 acres, about the same size as Central Park in New York City), jutting northward into Burrard Inlet and marking the entrance to Vancouver Harbour. Surrounding it is a 10km seawall popular with walkers, cyclists and rollerbladers.

The Teahouse, Stanley Park

From wilderness to park

Remarkable foresight on the part of Vancouver's city council in 1886 resulted in the creation of Stanley Park. The swampy peninsula was then a naval reserve where deer, bear, raccoon and cougar roamed along narrow trails and abandoned logging roads. The council petitioned the federal government to set it aside as a park.

The petition was granted, leaving only Deadman's Island as a naval base. So in 1888, the then Governor General of Canada, Lord Stanley, dedicated the park 'to the use and enjoyment of people of all colours, creeds and customs for all time'.

A park for all tastes

Today, about 8 million people a year come from all over Canada and the world to enjoy Stanley Park. Even on a warm summer day, visitors who do not want to mingle with the crowds can seek out the solitude of a shady trail.

Stanley Park is many things to many people. To youngsters, it is the sandy beach, a baby beluga whale, or a miniature railway. To teenagers, it is a trysting place and a playground for such sports as soccer, skateboarding, rollerblading and cycling.

To families, the park often means a leisurely Sunday picnic on a blanket under weeping willows. To the many elderly who live nearby in the West End concrete jungle, this urban oasis provides access to nature and the opportunity for a pleasant stroll around Lost Lagoon to feed the birds and squirrels.

The green oasis

The dense park forest consists mainly of cool conifers – red cedar, Douglas fir and hemlock. One old red cedar here measures 6m (20 feet) across and 64m (210 feet) tall. The deciduous underforest is mostly of broadleaved maples, vine maples and alders. The cultivated Rose Garden, which displays thousands of blooms every summer, adds a big splash of colour near the Georgia Street park entrance.

Park wildlife

There are few wild animals in the park today, except for the sealife in the aquarium, and the squirrels, raccoons and skunks around Lost Lagoon. Occasionally, a black-tailed deer swims over from the North Shore to enjoy a free lunch. The last cougar disappeared nearly 50 years ago.

The beavers have been removed from Beaver Lake, because their efficient sawmill and logging operations were destroying many trees and leaving others to fall on unsuspecting visitors. They also dug tunnels that undermined the miniature railway and penetrated the bison pen. After Easter every year, a suspicious number of domestic bunnies appear in the park, suggesting that some parents have given their children more than they can handle.

It was migratory birds, however, that introduced carp to the Lost Lagoon, named by poetess Pauline Johnson because its waters used to disappear at low tide. The water, now locked in by man-made devices, is fresh. The Lost Lagoon area is a bird sanctuary, home to cormorants, mergansers, scaup, ringbill, green wing-tail, shovelers, mallard and many other species of feathered friends.

A few hundred Canada geese also maintain residence here, and another thousand or so fly in for the winter. In spring, mother geese, ducks and swans parade proudly around with gaggles of young ones.

Bald eagles, which have several nests in the park, fly over Lost Lagoon and, on occasions, shamelessly grab an unsuspecting mallard for a meal, totally indifferent to horrified onlookers who have forgotten that Mother Nature is both creative and cruel.

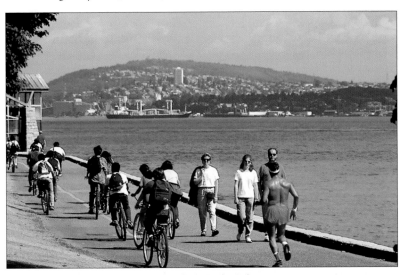

The seawall is a great place to get some exercise in Stanley Park

Stanley Park attractions

Shortly after the park opened in 1889, the warden adopted a black bear, which he kept tethered to a tree stump. Apparently, the local vicar's wife used to bring over household scraps to feed the bear. But one day the bear ignored the food and took a swipe at the lady's skirt. He was then banished to a bear pit, and it was decided to set aside an enclosed section of the park for wild animals.

White beluga whales never fail to draw attention at the Vancouver Aquarium

The zoo grew to house 400 animals representing 90 different species. However, it was shut down because people were concerned about the relatively small area the animals had to live in. All that remains is the Children's Farmyard, which affords a great opportunity for youngsters to hug and be nuzzled by dozens of domestic animals. As well as the usual rabbits and goats, this 'petting zoo' includes such unusual species as Jacob sheep, Vietnamese pot-bellied pigs and miniature cows, along with various reptiles and birds.

To see wild animals, visitors must now drive an hour east from downtown to the Vancouver Game Farm in Aldergrove (*tel: (604) 856 6825*), where giraffes, lions, tigers, camels, hippos and 100 other species roam a rangeland of 48 hectares (119 acres).

The Stanley Park Miniature Railway, which partly owes its existence to the terrific winds that uprooted thousands of trees and created an open area in the 1960s, has always carried more adults than children. Passengers ride in little canopied coaches pulled by a replica of the engine that led the first trans-continental train in to Vancouver in 1887. The 10-minute ride along the narrow rails goes through an avalanche tunnel and round a small artificial lake. *Tel: (604) 257 8530. Open: 5 June–5 Sept, daily 11am–5pm; Oct–May, weekends only 11am–5pm. Admission charge.*

Vancouver Aquarium

The Vancouver Aquarium is home to more than 9,000 aquatic creatures. A 5.5-m (18-foot) high bronze sculpture of a leaping killer whale, expertly crafted by Haida artist Bill Reid, marks the entrance.

Inside the aquarium, the more active denizens of the deep range from delicate seahorses to smiling crocodiles. Killer whales are no longer on display. The Marine Mammal Deck is a great viewing place. A wall-size viewing window shows playful sea otters cavorting above and below water. On the same deck is another area for harbour seals.

The Arctic Canada exhibition lets visitors look beneath the polar ice of the High Arctic at graceful white beluga whales; the big underwater windows make for excellent viewing.

Other sights and sounds of the far north, including fish with antifreeze genetically built in, are presented in a discovery centre within the aquarium.

The North Pacific Gallery and the Rufe Gibbs Hall have displays of such Canadian coastal water residents as giant octopuses, silvery salmon and waving sea anemones.

The humid Amazon Gallery provides pathways for strolling through a small tropical jungle, with banana and other equatorial trees where sloths hang lazily in the heat. Brightly coloured tropical birds flit among the tiny marmosets living in treetops, while in the water, other imported Amazon residents include anacondas, piranhas, stingrays and electric eels.

The Tropical Gallery features steely-eyed sharks, fish that glow in the dark, and rainbows of reef fishes whose families come from the clear blue waters of the Caribbean and Australia's Great Barrier Reef.

Children especially enjoy the tidal pools where they can touch anemones, chitons and starfish. School children frequently tour the zoo and aquarium on weekday mornings, so the afternoon is usually a less crowded time to visit.

The aquarium's Summer Speakers Series offers early-evening lectures by naturalists on a variety of topics, and there are daily Dive Shows and Meet the Trainer talks.

Stanley Park Aquarium. Tel: (604) 659 3400. Open: daily, mid-Sept–mid-June 10am–5.30pm; mid-June–mid-Sept 9.30am–7pm; Christmas & New Year's Day noon–5pm. Admission charge. Aquarium: www.vanaqua.org

A statue of the orca killer whale, no longer seen live at the Aquarium

By bike: the seawall

The Stanley Park Seawall must be one of the best urban cycle routes in the world. About 150 benches line the seawall. Several shops near the Georgia Street entrance to the park, a 10-minute walk from most downtown hotels, hire bicycles and tandems by the hour. The 10-km (6-mile) long paved pathway follows the perimeter of the 400-hectare (988-acre) peninsular park. The right side of the pathway, which is mostly level, is set aside for cyclists and rollerbladers. The trail runs anticlockwise and begins at Lost Lagoon. Walk bikes along the underpass and right to the seawall.

Allow about 2 hours.

1 Vancouver Rowing Club

Just past Km 0 is the Tudor-style Vancouver Rowing Club. Single sculls and eights skim Coal Harbour's sheltered waters where coal was discovered in the 1800s. Across the harbour, the city skyline is highlighted by the big white canvas sails of Canada Place. Almost opposite the Rowing Club stands a statue of Lord Stanley, a former Governor General of Canada who, in 1889, dedicated the park 'to the use and enjoyment of people of all colours, creeds and customs for all time'.

2 Nine O'Clock Gun

A little further along stands a statue of Scottish poet Robert Burns and another of Harry Jerome, once the world's fastest runner. The Nine O'Clock Gun, which once called herring fishermen home, still booms across the harbour every evening.

3 Brockton Point

A bright red-and-white-striped lighthouse marks Brockton Point, where fishermen cast their lines. Across Burrard Inlet brilliant yellow piles of sulphur await export. Behind lies Brockton Oval, a cinder jogging track encircling a summer cricket pitch which is used by rugby players in winter. A little further along, the bronze sculpture of *Girl in a wet suit* sits in the water near the shore, against the elegant sweep of the Lions Gate Bridge.

4 Lumberman's Arch

At Lumberman's Arch, near Km 3, grassy slopes overlook a water park for children. This was once the site of a Squamish native village, and tons of seashells from the midden were used to surface the first road in the park in 1888. It is a short cycle off the seawall to the aquarium and zoo (*see pp72–3*).

5 Prospect Point

Prospect Point, perched on a cliff, is the highest point in the park, where a cairn commemorates the SS *Beaver*, the pioneer steamship of the Pacific which sank nearby in 1888. You can see the huge pillars that support the Lions Gate Bridge, which stands 80m (262 feet) above the water and spans 170m (558 feet).

6 Siwash Rock

A little further on, Siwash Rock juts defiantly skyward from the sea. Often a grey gull clings to the small tree on top of a tuft of green on the 15-m (49-foot) high column of grey rock. The rock is the subject of an Indian legend. Millennia ago, a handsome young chief and his wife lived nearby. When their son was born the chief plunged into the waters to cleanse himself to ensure a spotless life for the newborn. At that moment giants in a canoe demanded that the chief forsake this ritual bath and go ashore. He refused, and they were so impressed by his love and devotion to the child, that they transformed him into Siwash Rock, to stand forever as a monument to Clean Fatherhood. The legend was recorded a century ago by Mohawk poet-princess Pauline Johnson, who is buried in a leafy glade nearby. A stone monument marks her grave.

7 Second Beach

Second Beach has a popular children's playground and a sandy beach, ideal for sunbathing and watching the sunset. On summer evenings, dancers take over the paved patio nearby. The cycle trail crosses the main road through the park, and passes a Japanese-style bridge crossing a willow-banked stream. In the surrounding meadow, Canada geese graze for grain. Beyond are a pitch-and-putt golf course, lawn bowling greens, tennis courts and a fine Mediterranean-style restaurant.

The trail continues over a humped bridge and follows the southern shore along Lost Lagoon to the start of the tour.

Unknown Vancouver

Although Vancouverites love their city, they sometimes take local treasures for granted, so visitors have to hunt to find them. Such local newspapers as the *Georgia Strait*, along with local radio and television stations, provide information on the area's life and leisure. Almost every weekend sees a variety of community events. At the spring dog parade, hundreds of Vancouverites walk their pets in Stanley Park. Libraries often hold readings by Canadian authors, and visitors may purchase a temporary card to borrow books.

A little BC eccentricity…

For an outdoor adventure, try picking strawberries, raspberries and blueberries in the Fraser Valley during the summer months. Salmonberries and blackberries can also be picked along many country roads and trails.

A great way to see the suburbs is to take in a garage sale on a weekend: this combines the opportunity for a bargain buy with an ideal informal meeting place. Local community newspapers list the sale venues. It is interesting to see what is sold and bought. People are very rarely in a hurry. It is, therefore, easy to strike up conversations. And you may get your Christmas shopping done early and at reduced prices.

Capilano Salmon Hatchery

Here you can watch salmon in various stages of growth in glass-fronted holding tanks. In the spawning season, the fish swim upstream and leap ladders into the hatchery.
4500 Capilano Park Rd, off Capilano Rd, in North Vancouver. Tel: (604) 666 1790.

Open: daily 8am–4pm; until 7 or 8pm in the summer. Free admission.

Resort Semiahmoo

Although Vancouver is surrounded by water, there are no beachfront resorts. Drive an hour south to Blaine, Washington, to the Inn at Semiahmoo. Great beach walks with gulls, herons and bald eagles; good seafood at Packers Lounge; a swimming pool, and a golf course which is a three-time *Golf Magazine* Silver Award winner.
On the Semiahmoo Spit in Blaine.
Tel: (800) 770 7992; www.semiahmoo.com

Vancouver Flea Market

Bargain shopping is a favourite pastime in Vancouver – as can be seen at the suburban garage sales – and the flea market is a mecca for junk-hunters. At this weekend event, both junk and genuine bargains fill the display tables.
703 Terminal Ave, close to the Main St SkyTrain. Tel: (604) 685 0666. Open: Sat, Sun & holidays 9am–5pm.

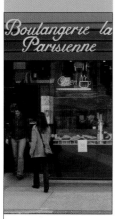

Boulangerie on Mainland

Yaletown

Yaletown, the trendiest downtown area, centres around Mainland Street between Nelson and Davie streets. Just over a century ago, this neighbourhood was rainforest wilderness – until 1887, when the Canadian Pacific Railway moved its operations from the little town of Yale to this spot on the north shore of False Creek. A shanty town of wood-frame homes, boarding houses and hotels developed here. One of the original wooden homes, the Perry Linden House, still stands at 1021 Richards Street.

From the early 20th century, brick warehouses replaced the wooden structures. By the 1950s, most residents had moved to the suburbs. In recent years, creative people have been converting the old warehouses into work and retail space, resulting in wonderful walking streets lined with shops, galleries and restaurants.

The growing selection of stores specialises in art supplies, coffee, flowers, designer and discounted clothing, sports and legal attire, and pricey home furnishings.

The Yaletown Galleria, at 1080 Mainland, houses three floors of offices and shops, overlooking a central atrium. The shops include the Light Resource, where a lighting specialist makes cappuccinos for customers, along with several other showrooms which sell furniture and accessories ranging from *étagères* to oriental urns.

Mangiamo (*1116 Mainland; tel: (604) 687 1116*), recently voted one of Vancouver's favourite restaurants, features both Italian cuisine and décor.

Cambie Street offers half a dozen interesting art galleries and Granville Island has speciality shops such as Maiwa Handprints, a fibre arts store.

Yaletown is not too glossy yet, although chic condos are sprouting around its perimeter. It is the kind of place where an advertising executive in a Gucci jacket might carry work home in a dustbin bag. Enjoy it quickly, before it changes.

For more information see *www.yaletowninfo.com*

Death by Chocolate, Yaletown

Vancouver
suburbs: south

STEVESTON

A half-hour drive (32km/20 miles) south
from downtown Vancouver is Steveston
at the mouth of the mighty Fraser. The
river boasts the biggest salmon run in
North America, and Steveston has the
largest fleet of commercial fishing vessels
on Canada's West Coast.

Garry Point Park

A five-minute walk west lies sandy,
windswept Garry Point Park. A tiny
Oriental garden, beside the broad
walking path, commemorates the arrival
of the first Japanese immigrants more
than a century ago.

Around Moncton Street

Seafood restaurants, marine supply
stores, antique shops and such shopping
delights as The Country Garden Mouse
(*tel: (604) 272 4752*), which stocks a
selection of Canadian crafts; the Canoe
Pass Gallery (*tel: (604) 272 0095*), which
sells traditional Coast Indian art; and
the Riverside Gallery (*tel: (604) 274
1414*), which displays work by the owner
and other artists.

Steveston Museum

A collection of fishing, farming and
blacksmith tools used by early Japanese
settlers. Some rooms in the two-storey
1906 structure have been restored with
period furniture.
*3811 Moncton Street. Open: Mon–Sat
9.30am–1pm, 1.30–5pm.*
Tel: (604) 271 6868.

Vancouver suburbs

Suburbs: north

Across Burrard Inlet and English Bay lies Vancouver's North Shore, backed by the rugged Coast Range mountains. Rivers, creeks and canyons meander down forested slopes, cut through clusters of houses, high-rises and businesses, and terminate along park-lined shores. Scenic coastal and mountain drives, a dozen shopping areas, a few hotels, 250 restaurants, and other businesses cater to the 200,000 North Shore residents and a much greater number of visitors (*www.cnv.org*).

Cypress, Grouse and Seymour mountains, visible from almost every vantage point in Vancouver, dominate the scene. So near yet so far from downtown, these city mountains provide a recreational paradise, particularly for picnics and hiking in summer and skiing in winter. When the clouds disperse, various vantage points provide spectacular views of downtown, the Gulf Islands, the American San Juan Islands and the eternal snows of distant Mount Baker.

The Capilano River and Grouse Mountain

Grouse Mountain, 1,220m (4,003 feet) high, is a mere 15 minutes by car from downtown Vancouver to the big parking lot below the Skyride. The aerial gondola then takes 10 minutes to transport 100 passengers at a time up through sweeping vistas to fresh, crisp mountain air, winding trails, alpine meadows and a superb ski area.

The most developed of the city mountains, Grouse offers a variety of top options. You can hop on a helicopter (*tel: (604) 270 1484, toll free (800) 665 4354; www.helijet.com*) and fly high across Capilano Canyon and between the peaks of The Lions. Or you can enjoy such other attractions as horse-drawn wagon rides, an adventure playground for the children, the Bistro Patio for relaxing, the elegant Grouse Nest Restaurant for high dining, and, in July, the hang-gliding championships, when flyers jump off the mountain and glide down towards the city. A 60-minute show at the

The breathtaking aerial gondola ride up to Grouse Mountain

THE LEGEND OF THE TWO SISTERS

Renamed The Lions by the British, these twin peaks rise to 1,646m (5,400 feet) at the northern end of the Cypress Provincial Park wilderness. A long time ago, as a great Capilano chief prepared to celebrate the coming of age of his twin daughters, a powerful northerly tribe declared war. But the daughters persuaded their father to invite the hostile Indians to their feast, and this *potlatch* festival of peace brought friendship to the tribes. The chief decided to make his daughters immortal, and lifted them to these lofty twin peaks to stand forever as symbols of peace and friendship.

mountain-top Theatre In The Sky tells a high-tech tale of a First Nation carver mystically transformed into an eagle, and of Vancouver's change from a frontier outpost to a thriving metropolis in less than a century.

On the way down, there are several stops worth making. The enormous **Cleveland Dam**, built about 40 years ago, divides the river to create Capilano Lake, which provides the water supply for the city. At the **Capilano Salmon Hatchery** (*tel: (604) 666 1790*) from July to October, returning salmon leap ladders into the hatchery, and a display shows coho, steelhead and chinook in various stages of development.

The Capilano Suspension Bridge (*tel: (604) 985 7474; www.capbridge.com*), the world's oldest suspension footbridge, was originally built in 1889. The wire rope and wood structure sways and flaps 70m (230 feet) above the rushing waters of the river below. The bridge stretches 137m (449 feet) across the steep canyon, providing access to nature trails meandering through an old-growth forest. Stop for a snack at the Bridge Restaurant across the street, where the benevolent and playful spirit of a former resident sometimes entertains, or check out Treetops, the newest attraction.
For more information see www.grousemountain.com

The Capilano Suspension Bridge

NORTH SHORE MOUNTAINS
Cypress Provincial Park

Northwest of Vancouver, overlooking Howe Sound to the west, Cypress Provincial Park provides spectacular views over the city to Mount Baker and southwest to Vancouver Island and the Gulf Islands. Excellent cross-country ski trails and good downhill runs attract Vancouverites every day and evening in winter. In summer, the main attraction is the network of hiking trails. Some, such as the Yew Lake circuit, are suitable for novices, while the Crest Trail challenges even the experts.

It takes about 20 minutes to drive to the park along the Cypress Parkway from the exit on Upper Levels Highway (Highway 1/99). The end of the road is marked by a large parking area, a cafeteria, a shop and the park administration building, where brochures illustrating the trails are available.

The forest comprises mostly evergreens, such as Douglas and amabilis fir, which thrive on this rainy coast. Deciduous trees include alders, maples and the flowering dogwood, whose neat white blossom is the provincial flower. Ferns and mosses, fed by stumps and fallen and ageing trees, flourish, and marsh marigold, skunk cabbage and salmonberries also brighten the landscape. Black bears love the berries, so be sure to give them right of way. Watchful eyes sometimes see deer feeding on the open slopes along the road. The boldest bird is the whisky jack, which lands right on picnic tables, while chickadees, nuthatches, crossbills and Steller's jays forage in the forest.

Tel: (604) 926 5612; www.cypressmountain.com

Mount Seymour Provincial Park

This park encompasses 3,500 hectares (8,649 acres) of wilderness, including Mount Elsay and Mount Bishop, as well as Mount Seymour (1,450m/4,757 feet). It contains old-growth fir, western red and yellow cedar,

There are lots of ski options in BC

The city of Vancouver against the backdrop of Mount Seymour

and hemlock, with carpets of alpine flowers in open areas. Coyotes and deer appear sometimes, close to the highway, and hares, Douglas squirrels and martens sometimes skirt the hiking trails. An occasional black bear or cougar is sometimes sighted in the back country. The guided tours and displays in the Seymour Demonstration Forest (*tel: (604) 987 1273*) are an excellent way to learn about local flora and fauna, rainforests and fisheries.

The winding 13-km (8-mile) highway up Seymour ends at parking lot 4, near the cafeteria and chair lift. The Goldie Lake/Flower Lake Trail, a nordic ski route in winter, provides an easy and relatively flat one-hour loop, although a dozen other recommended walks are listed in the brochure available in the cafeteria. Part-way down the highway, a two-hour walk along the Baden-Powell Trail leads down through thick forest and across ravines to the village of Deep Cove, on the Indian Arm, which has a sandy beach and a canoe rental shop. *Tel: (604) 986 2261; www.mountseymour.com*

Parks on Indian Arm

A water taxi runs across Indian Arm from **Deep Cove** to Belcarra Regional Park, which shelters Sasamat Lake, one of the warmest in the region. Cates Park, where the waters of Indian Arm and Burrard Inlet meet, is popular with scuba divers. A 15-m (49-foot) long war canoe, carved in an unusual chequerboard design, is displayed in the park. The nearby Malcolm Lowry Walk provides a peaceful 10-minute stroll through the leafy forest and back along the shell-strewn shore. *www.deepcovebc.com*

WHISTLER

Named after the call of the hoary marmot, one of the first inhabitants of the area, Whistler is a top-class winter sports centre that continues to receive accolades from skiers from all over the world. And getting there is half the fun.

The Sea to Sky Highway

Appropriately called the Sea to Sky Highway, the road to Whistler fringes fiord-like Howe Sound. Here, rugged rainforest and sheer rock faces, sculpted by glaciers during the last Ice Age, ascend to meadows blanketed in summer with Indian paintbrushes and other alpine flowers, and in winter with snow.

A good picnic place along the road is **Porteau Cove**, which also offers good swimming, snorkelling, scuba diving, boating and fishing. At Britannia Beach, the **BC Mining Museum**, once the largest copper producer in the British Empire and now a National Historic Site, offers underground tours in little electric trains, and an intriguing display of old mining equipment (*tel: (604) 896 2233, toll free (800) 896 4044; www.bcmuseumofmining.org. Open: mid-May–mid-Oct 9am–5.30pm. Admission charge*).

The next stop should be **Shannon Falls**; *www.britishcolumbia.com/parksandtrails/parks*. BC's third-highest waterfall thunders down a 335-m (1,099-foot) cliff following the trail of a slithering sea serpent, according to the local legend.

A few kilometres beyond the falls, the logging town of **Squamish** is famous as a rock-climbing centre. The Stawamus Chief, a 652-m (2,139-foot) high granite

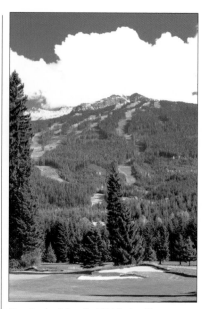
Stunning backdrop for Whistler's golf course

monolith, is second in size in the world, after the Rock of Gibraltar. Another hour's drive past reflecting lakes and through small open valleys and forest, lies Whistler.

Whistler: the mountain playground

Whistler Village is nestled between twin mountain peaks, Whistler and Blackcomb, in the Coast Range. The village is a cluster of hotels, shops, condominiums, restaurants and cobbled walkways, constructed in a mixed West Coast and imitation European style.

A five-minute walk from the village square leads to the ski lifts which service the largest ski area and the two longest vertical drops on the continent: Blackcomb, 1,609m (5,279 feet), and

Whistler, 1,530m (5,020 feet). The resort also has the most extensive high-speed ski-lift system in the world, with a total of 30 lifts, including three gondolas and nine quad chairs. About a quarter of the 200 downhill runs are tailored to experts, another quarter to beginners, and the rest are for intermediate skiers. Cross-country trails skirt the golf course and Lost Lake. After the warm spring sun melts the snows of winter, avid skiers head to the Horstman Glacier and share the lifts with mountain bikers, who ride down the now-gravel trails that skiers slalom in winter. Overhead, paragliders float down to the village below.

Whistler also offers an 18-hole golf course, hiking, horse riding, canoeing, river rafting, windsurfing and fishing. Musicians, magicians, clowns, comedians and jugglers entertain every day in the streets from mid-June to September. Major festivals feature country and blues in July, classical music in August and jazz in September.

Accommodation varies, from the luxurious 343-room Château Whistler, the largest château-style property built in Canada for a century, to the rustic Whistler Campground and RV Park. *Tel: 1 800 WHISTLER (toll free); www.tourismwhistler.com*

How to get there
You can travel to Whistler, 120km (75 miles) north of Vancouver, by Helijet (*tel: (800) 665 4354; www.helijet.com*); Maverick Coach Lines (*tel: (604) 255 1171; www.maverickcoach.com*); or drive yourself, which takes about two hours nonstop. For further information see: *www.tourismwhistler.com or www.whistleronline.com*

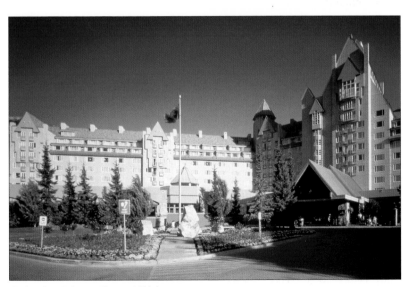
The luxurious Fairmont Chateau Whistler

Vancouver is a little like The Sleeping Beauty – blessed by the good fairies at birth with great natural beauty everywhere you look. The city rests at the foot of a range of mountains and looks out to the ocean with deep inlets cutting into the land. Parks and gardens are scattered everywhere through the city, and pristine rainforest and wilderness lie just behind the last row of houses on the North Shore. Is it any wonder, then, that Vancouverites coexist harmoniously (most of the time) with critters from the forest?

In North Vancouver, signs in the parks warn of wandering bears, and local dogs stroll along wearing 'bear bells'. It's not unusual for a local matron to step outside onto the doorstep for her morning paper and see a bear walking up the driveway. Most of the time these natural encounters are uneventful, but not too long ago a cougar wandered into Victoria and was seen prowling around the car park of the city's most famous hotel. Raccoons seem to hang out wherever there's a small stand of natural park, and in the city they can be a real nuisance on 'garbage day' along with legions of chipmunks, skunks and squirrels. The city's most famous park – the 440-hectare (1,087-acre) Stanley Park – is a thickly wooded tract of cedar, hemlock and fir and has its own battalion of raccoons that will shamelessly beg for French fries or popcorn. Park officials discourage visitors from feeding these beggars since

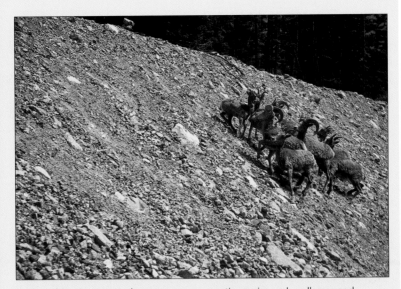

they can bite. Even more dangerous are the minefields of poop left by the park's beautiful but messy Canada geese.

In the Fraser Valley to the east of the city and beyond, you can see fields of ordinary farm animals but also more exotic species such as llamas and alpacas that are being raised as pets, for their wool or as guide animals. On the Gulf Islands and on Vancouver Island deer can be so plentiful they are considered pests, and on a train ride further into the province there's a good chance of catching a herd of bighorn sheep grazing by the tracks.

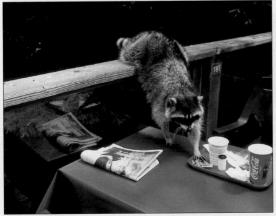

Vancouver's many pockets of wilderness, whether public or private, are a delight for animal lovers

Walk: Bowen Island

Bowen Island is located northwest of Vancouver – a 20-minute ferry ride from Horseshoe Bay to Snug Cove. It is a wonderful day trip from Vancouver. This lush, green, bowl-shaped isle, capped by 760-m (2,493-foot) Mount Gardner, has long been a holiday hideaway for Vancouverites. *Allow a day for the trip.*

By car the drive takes half an hour; head northwest along Georgia Street, across the Lions Gate Bridge and follow the ferry signs west along the Upper Levels Highway. There is usually ample parking in Horseshoe Bay, except on holiday weekends. A car is not necessary on the island; board the ferry as a foot passenger.

As the ferry rounds the point from Horseshoe Bay into Queen Charlotte Sound, the Lions and the Howe Sound Crest mountains appear dramatically outlined against the sky. South across the water lies little Passage Island, Point

Atkinson lighthouse and, across English Bay, Point Grey.

From the ferry dock in Snug Cove, it is a three-minute walk along Government Road to the commercial centre of the island.

This main square has a couple of pubs, restaurants with flower-decked patios, craft shops, bakeries, and the restored Union Steamship Company Store, now the local library. The Visitor Information Centre is right behind the library.

Visitors travel via BC Ferries from Horseshoe Bay

Detour right before the store where a short, tree-lined road leads to a freshwater lagoon on one side and the calm waters of Deep Bay on the other. Opposite Cardena Drive, a green sign indicates a leafy trail that marks the entrance to Crippen Regional Park and the Killarney Lake Trail.

It is a 6-km (4-mile) round trip. The trail is wide and fairly flat, except for a few steep sections. For a leisurely stroll, allow about two hours.

A few minutes along the trail, the sound of plunging Terminal Creek announces two fish ladders zigzagging up the rocky hillside beside the creek. During October and November, salmon that went to sea after being raised in a nearby hatchery return after two or three years to leap the ladders upstream and spawn in the waters they came from.

The trail, flanked by leafy screens of trees, emerges on to Miller Road. About 100m (328 feet) to the right, the trail continues on the other side. A second-growth forest of red cedars, hemlocks and maples towers over a tangled undergrowth where huge stumps still remain as reminders of earlier logging.

The trail crosses Magee Road to the Killarney Lake Loop Trail, where bikes and horses are not allowed. The main trail heads north around the lake to a gravel beach with picnic tables, wash-rooms and a small swimming area. The trail climbs slightly to join a broad boardwalk over a marsh where Labrador tea, bog laurel, sweet gale bushes and the carnivorous sundew plant thrive. In early summer brilliant yellow skunk cabbage, which smells like it sounds, glows in the underbrush. Blue herons hunch patiently in the shallow water, waiting for dinner to swim by. The trail meanders on, with frequent views of the lake and the forested foothills around Mount Gardner.

Follow the signs back to Snug Cove to catch the ferry back to the mainland.

From downtown Vancouver, take the Blue Bus (tel: (604) 985 7777) on Georgia St, which runs every half-hour to Horseshoe Bay. Allow an hour for the bus trip. Bus No 250 follows scenic Marine Drive through West Vancouver and Bus No 257 follows the highway. Most visitors arrive aboard BC Ferries Howe Sound Queen (tel: 1-888-BCFERRY; www.bcferries.com). For more information, tel: (250) 947 9024; fax: (250) 947 0633; www.bowenisland.org

Suburbs: west

Mention West Vancouver and most Canadians conjure up images of sprawling, million-dollar waterfront mansions backed by park-like gardens, and patio drives filled with Mercedes and Jaguars. It is true that the municipality's 40,000 residents do boast the highest per capita income in Canada. The most well-known luxurious residential area is called The British Properties. But many small clapboard cottages, built as summer homes long before the Guinness family built the Lions Gate Bridge in 1938, still survive here untouched by developers, and are valued at prices far lower than the current value of the land they occupy.

Point Atkinson Lighthouse

West Vancouver is not the Wild West. About 20 per cent of West Vaners are pensioned senior citizens. There is little crime and no industry. The suburb snakes for 20km (12 miles) along the north shore of English Bay from the Lions Gate Bridge to Horseshoe Bay, and climbs about 5km up the slope towards Cypress Mountain. Although there are 60 public parks for 15,000 homes, most back gardens would look like parks to New Yorkers. Once people have lived here, they say they would not want to live anywhere else in Canada, even though commuters encounter frequent waits in summer to cross the bridge to the big city.

For browsing or buying, West Vancouver has the Park Royal Shopping Centre and a good range of little stores in Ambleside village and in the one block between 24th and 25th Street called Dundarave. Visitors can also enjoy fishing, golfing, tennis at free public courts, lawn bowling, swimming and exercise at several fitness circuits.

Ferry building

Built in 1913, this heritage building, which is now a waterfront gallery, was once a meeting place for residents arriving from and leaving for downtown Vancouver. The adjacent waterfront park, known as Ambleside Landing, offers a view of Prospect Point in Stanley Park, and features a fountain sculpture and a fishing pier complete with cleaning table.
1414 Argyle Ave. Tel: (604) 925 7290. Open: Tue–Thur, Sat & Sun 10am–6pm; Fri 10am–8pm.

Gertrude Lawson Museum

This old ballast-stone house was built in 1940 by Gertrude Lawson, daughter of the Father of West Vancouver, businessman John Lawson. It is now a museum relating the history of the area. The unusual stone façade of the house echoes the architectural character of the grand homes of Scotland which Ms Lawson greatly admired. The stones are

themselves believed to have come from New Zealand as ballast on timber trading ships.
680 17th St. Tel: (604) 925 7295. Open: Tue–Sun 11am–5pm; winter Tue–Sat noon–4.30pm. Admission charge.

Parks and walkways

Gardens, parks and walkways are everywhere. Ambleside Park is a great place to see residents walking their dogs. The spectacular 2-km (1¼-mile) paved Seawalk has a fenced-off trail for four-footed friends. The best beach is the little one near Dundarave Pier, between 14th and Bellevue, where a concession stand at the bottom of 25th Ave serves the best cheeseburgers in BC in the summer. This is also a popular place for summer crabbing and fishing. Westward, a pebbled shore strewn with driftwood, is a great place for beachcombing. Caulfield Park, which has a forested path along the waterfront, is famous for its flush toilets!

Lighthouse Park, a treasure hidden away further west along Marine Drive, has a labyrinth of trails through an enchanted forest of giant Douglas firs, pines, hemlocks and arbutus trees, recognisable by their smooth, peeling rust-red bark. The Point Atkinson Lighthouse, built in 1912, is one of the few working lighthouses left in the province. The promontory just west of the lighthouse offers views of freighters anchored in English Bay, Point Grey and the mountains of Vancouver Island.

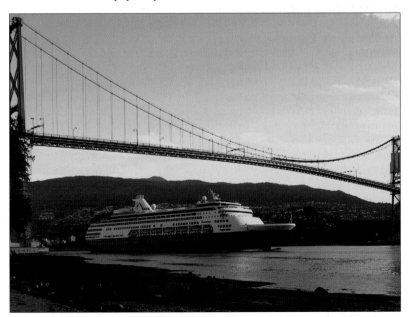

Lions Gate Bridge spans Burrard Inlet, linking downtown with the North Shore

Suburbs: east

LOWER MAINLAND
Fort Langley

An hour's drive east from Vancouver's chrome and glass high-rises is the historic little village of Fort Langley, the site of the original fort and fur-trading post where BC began. It was here that BC was declared a Crown Colony in 1858.

Fort Langley village has, so far, escaped the contrived charm which often accompanies historical reconstructions. This can be attributed to the fact that most of its quaint clapboard churches, antique shops and false-fronted buildings are original.

Near the fort, the **BC Farm Museum** (*9131 King St. Tel: (604) 888 2273*) houses a comprehensive collection of steam tractors, stump pullers, ploughs, reapers, harvesters, buckboards, a working sawmill and a vintage Tiger Moth plane – the first crop duster in the province.

The **Langley Centennial Museum**, next door, displays numerous Coast Salish Indian artefacts and a selection of 19th-century pioneer crafts and furnishings.

Fort Langley National Historic Site

First built in 1839, Fort Langley was once the Hudson's Bay Company's most important provisioning post in the Pacific Northwest, and has been reconstructed to re-create the past. Within the palisaded high wooden walls, the Big House, the bastion, a cooperage and carpentry shop, and a blacksmith's forge have been rebuilt. The storehouse, the only original structure on site, is stacked with furs, clothing, trapping equipment, trading goods and other supplies used by fur traders, gold miners, Indians and other 19th-century residents.

Interpreters in period costumes demonstrate pioneer life at the fort. Some are blacksmiths fashioning tools; some are coopers building barrels, which were once used to ship salmon and other foodstuffs from the fort; and some bake salmon and bannock in open outdoor ovens for sampling.

Other interpreters present talks and organise games to help children

THE HUDSON'S BAY COMPANY

This company of English adventurers formed in 1670, during the reign of King Charles II, to trade in North America throughout the lands that drained into Hudson's Bay.

The commercial empire that grew out of it began with a few shiploads of British goods being traded for furs, and eventually covered more than 10 per cent of the surface of the earth. After numerous dramatic struggles, a merger with the North West Company took place in 1821.

When Canada became a country, the Hudson's Bay Company gave up its trade monopoly, but retained its forts and trading posts. Eventually, a chain of Hudson's Bay department stores was built in western Canada and still exists today. Small Bay stores remain as the commercial centres of several remote settlements scattered throughout the Canadian Arctic.

enjoy learning local history. Coast Salish Natives from the neighbouring MacMillan Island band often work at the fort constructing canoes, carving paddles and making jewellery.

The Big House replicates the original building which was pulled down in 1886. The refurbished parlour suggests the relative luxury the chief trader and his family enjoyed, and an intriguing diary displayed in the big hall describes early life at the fort.

Brigade Days, held in early August, re-enact the fur brigades arriving to trade at Fort Langley after weeks of canoeing south through networks of rivers. Douglas Day, in mid-November, is another colourful ceremony, which commemorates the inauguration of BC.

The Friends of the Fort gift shop stocks a variety of souvenirs, including reproductions of old trading goods from the fort.

23433 Mavis St. Tel: (604) 513 4777. www.pc.gc.ca/fortlangley. Open: daily, by appointment only.

The Native riverboat trip

A pleasant way to visit Fort Langley is aboard *The Native*, a working replica of a late 19th-century paddlewheeler. This 100-passenger vessel follows the Fraser River upstream from New Westminster to Fort Langley. The four-hour journey traces the route taken by fortune hunters, fur traders, miners, merchants, millionaires and stagecoach robbers during the 19th century. Native Indians also canoed the route while fishing, hunting and trapping. The excursion is narrated, with extracts by early explorers. The company runs both lunch and dinner cruises.

139–810 Quayside, New Westminster. Tel: (604) 525 4465; www.vancouverpaddlewheeler.com

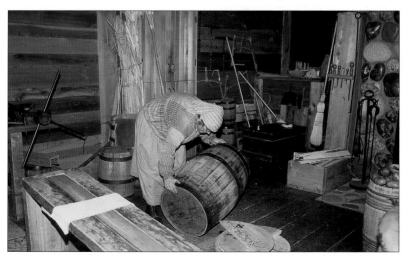

A costumed interpreter at Fort Langley

HARRISON HOT SPRINGS

These hot springs were discovered rather dramatically during the 1850s when a clumsy prospector was tipped out of his canoe into Harrison Lake. He was dumbfounded to find the water not frigid, but warm. Word spread and, for later prospectors on the gold rush trail, Harrison Hot Springs became a popular stopover site.

Although Harrison Hot Springs Hotel is today in the luxury category, anyone can enjoy such specialities as lobster mousse or poached salmon in the restaurant and look out at the lake. There is also plenty of less expensive hotel, motel and campground accommodation. Other restaurants line the lakeshore.

Shoppers and browsers can enjoy a range of shops offering everything from video rentals, camping supplies and Canadiana to the Christmas decorations sold year-round in the cosy Holly Tree Place.

Soothing spring waters

Two springs percolate from the base of nearby mountains. A sulphur spring, about two-thirds sodium sulphate and sodium chloride, flows out at 68°C (154°F). A potash spring, with potassium chloride and sodium sulphate making up more than half its mineral content, enters the lake at 71°C (160°F). Both spring waters also contain lime and magnesium sulphates, sulphurated hydrogen and bicarbonates of lime and iron. To see the springs bubbling up from their source, walk westward along the dyke beside the lake and past the hotel.

A pipe system carries the mineral waters to the hotel and public pools, for which there is an admission charge. The water is stored in huge tanks and cooled to 38°C (100°F), the perfect temperature for a soothing soak. Massages are available.

Outdoor activities and sport

The town of Harrison Hot Springs offers a great variety of activities for lovers of the outdoors. Boaters enjoy exploring the lake, which stretches 60km north, but watch for strong thermal winds which may rise rapidly shortly after noon on a summer day. The morning calm is great for waterskiing, and the afternoon winds are great for windsurfing. Other outdoor options include golf, tennis, cycling, croquet, horseshoes and shuffleboard.

Numerous walking and hiking trails provide easy access to the forests and mountains. The easiest one, about 2km (1 1/4 miles) long, follows the lake from the Harrison Hot Springs Hotel to the boat launch and around the lagoon, while the Campbell Lake Trail, which requires more than four hours, rises a challenging 600m to a beautiful mountain lake.

The Sasquatch Daze in May, Days of Wine & Roses in June and the Sandsculpture Competition in early September attract many visitors to Harrison Hot Springs every year. The record for the world's tallest sandcastle was set here in 1990.

There is a parade of gaily lighted boats on the lake during the evening of 1 July, Canada Day. The week-long Festival of the Arts, later in July, features

a spectrum of artistic expression in music, dance, theatre and visual art, and artefacts. A special day set aside for children includes storytellers, face-painting, workshops and other activities, and a writers' evening offers readings with Canadian authors.
Tel: (604) 796 3664; www.harrison.ca, www.harrisonfestival.com

Minter Gardens
Tucked away a few metres west off Yale Road, just after the turn-off north from Highway 1 to Harrison Hot Springs, are the Minter Gardens. Pathways wind through 11 hectares (27 acres) of sights, sounds, fragrances, textures and tastes.

In springtime, tulips, daffodils, hyacinths, primulas, rhododendrons and azaleas blaze with colour. Summer brings a prize display of annuals, and autumn presents a shower of falling leaves in green, gold and red, backdropped by 2,134-m (7,001-foot) Mount Cheam. Other highlights include the Rose Garden, which blossoms most of the year; topiaries of southern belles and northern deer; a rare collection of Penjing rock bonsai; and a fragrance trail for the blind.
Tel: (604) 794 7191, toll free 1 888 646 8377; www.mintergardens.com. Open: Apr–Oct 9am–sunset. Admission charge. Free parking.

Minter Gardens is a riot of flowers in the summer

PEACE ARCH PARK

Canada, the second-largest country in area on earth (after Russia), and the USA have the longest, undefended international border in the world, stretching 6,500km (4,039 miles) from the Atlantic Ocean to the Pacific. Shared by both countries, the Peace Arch Park at the southern end of Highway 99 in BC may be one of the most beautiful border crossings anywhere.

A monument to peace

The idea of a peace arch was conceived by the late Samuel Hill of Seattle to commemorate a permanent peace between Canada and the USA. While president of the Pacific Highway Association, Hill, a road builder and Quaker, proposed that an arch be constructed at the centenary of the signing of the Treaty of Ghent in 1814. The treaty marked the end of the War of 1812 between Great Britain and the USA, resolving the ongoing conflict between the two powers at that time. The Peace Arch, the first such structure in the world, became a reality in 1921 and marked the 300th anniversary of the sailing of the Pilgrim Fathers to America.

Built of concrete reinforced with steel, in Greek Doric style, the arch was designed to vibrate but not crack in case of an earthquake. The gleaming white open portal, which stands about 30m high, flies the Canadian and American flags side by side. Across the top on the American side is the inscription 'Children of a Common Mother'. The Canadian side reads 'Brethren Dwelling Together in Unity'.

Two iron gates span the opening that leads from one country to the other. Here children and adults from both countries like to stand, with one foot planted on Canadian soil, the other in the USA. In a celebration held in early June every year, children from both countries meet here and file through the portal and exchange flags. Over the west gate is written '1814 – Open for One Hundred Years – 1914' and over the east 'May These Gates Never Be Closed'.

Originally incorporated into the Canadian side was a beam from the SS *Beaver*, which in 1836 became the first steamship to enter the Pacific Ocean. A beam of wood from the hull of *The Mayflower*, the ship that carried the Pilgrim Fathers to America in 1621, was embedded into the American side. These relics have since been removed and stored elsewhere for future generations.

A garden of harmony

During the 1920s, some peace lovers banded together to raise funds to purchase land surrounding the Peace Arch for a park. BC schoolchildren responded, some with only a penny, others with as much as 10 cents. More than $2,000 was raised, quite a lot in those days. The money was applied to the purchase of a portion of the property. Other funds were eventually found and 9 hectares (22 acres) were set aside as the **Peace Arch Park**. The 7 hectares (17 acres) that make up the Washington State Peace Arch Park were eventually acquired in a similar fashion.

Today, the Peace Arch serves as a symbol to remind all passing by that neighbours can live together in peace. The portal is the centrepiece for the surrounding broad green lawns, flower gardens, rockeries, playgrounds, picnic areas, shelters and kitchens that have been built on both sides over the years. The Canadian side features a wooden gazebo, a lily pond and a rectangle of red and white blossoms representing the Canadian flag. To the west, a cliff overlooks the old Burlington Northern Railway line and the waters of Semiahmoo Bay, which wash the shores of both countries.

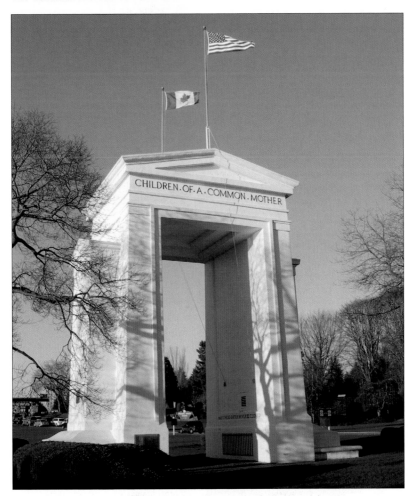

The symbolic open portal that bridges the national boundaries of Canada and the USA

When most people think of BC they envisage a land blanketed in greenery. The Lower Mainland region does tend to remain eternally leafy, thanks to the temperate climate and abundant rains.

It is usually March when the first crocuses, daffodils, tulips and hyacinths burst forth. Bold umbrellas of pink unfold on Japanese cherry trees along city streets; magnolias and camellias bloom in delicate whites and pinks, and the japonica bushes open bright clusters of flowers resembling apple blossoms. Forsythia shrubs produce golden streamers and wisterias wind long tassels of purple along building walls. Yellow skunk cabbages, which smell like they sound, brighten dank forest areas in Stanley Park.

In June, azaleas and rhododendrons, dressed in brilliant hues of pink, salmon, coral and crimson, announce the advent of summer. Roses bloom in town and country gardens, and wild lupins brighten the roadsides. Dahlias, delphiniums, phlox, asters and poppies share the summer sun with sweet peas, gladioli, freesias, zinnias, marigolds and nasturtiums, while fuchsias and busy Lizzies thrive in the shade. Moss-packed hanging baskets sport trailing lobelias and verbenas, mingled with petunias and pelargoniums.

The late summer display includes snapdragons, primroses, wallflowers and Canterbury bells. As the golden autumn leaves fall from the trees, irises, cat-tails (or reedmace) and marsh marigolds begin to flower near ponds and lakes.

Even the grey winter is brightened by flowering plants. Clumps of white and pink heather border lawns, while window boxes appear colourful with winter pansies and curly kale. Some roses, along with the pretty blossoms of the winter-flowering plum and the yellow trumpets of winter jasmine, smile right through a short snowfall. Holly outside and poinsettias inside follow the Christmas tradition of red and green. Red-osier dogwoods, the bright yellow twigs of Siberian dogwood and clusters of bright pink berries on the spindleberry bush also liven the winter landscape.

Whatever the season may be, BC's gardens and parks are always in full bloom

Vancouver's islands

Almost 200 islands of all shapes and sizes lie between the Lower Mainland and Vancouver Island (*see map pp104–5*). Some of these Gulf Islands offer superb natural scenery, outdoor activities, accommodation and food. Although locals love the quiet winters, the islands are much livelier in summer when visitors come from all over the world for the spectacular water views, the balmy climate, the abundant sunshine and the gentle lifestyle.

For more information visit www.islands.bc.ca

Basking in the sun on
Saltspring Island

GULF ISLANDS

The six major inhabited Gulf Islands are Saltspring, North and South Pender, Galiano, Mayne and Saturna. Saltspring is the most developed and the most densely populated. But Mayne, which is not the principal island, is preferred by many visitors. About 8km by 5km (5 miles by 3 miles) in area, Mayne Island has only 900 year-round residents. They are mostly artists and artisans, a few business people, and others who have retired to enjoy a leisurely island lifestyle.

Like the other Gulf Islands, Mayne is mainly bays and beaches, and gentle wooded hills of arbutus, Douglas fir, alder, cedar and brilliant bursts of broom, although early settlers did clear some land for farming.

Popular activities include swimming, scuba diving, fishing, canoeing, kayaking, clam digging, beachcombing, hiking and cycling.

The Gulf Islands are popular precisely because there is little organised activity. On Mayne, Blue Vista (*tel: (250) 539 2463, toll free (877) 535 2424*) does rent out kayaks and bikes, and leads interpretive kayak tours. Mayne Island kayak, canoe & bike rentals (*tel: (250) 539 5599*) also rents and has guided tours and instruction. Most Mayne roads are hilly, but asphalted. The nearby Produce Market, Trading Post and Deli pack picnic lunches.

Most of the Gulf Islands are accessible year-round via BC Ferries (*tel: 1 888 BCFERRY or (250) 386 343; www.bcferries.com*) and Harbour Air (*toll free (800) 665 0212; www.harbour-air.com*). Ferries to the islands leave Tsawwassen on the mainland 30km (19 miles) south of Vancouver. Many boaters prefer to visit in their own craft, finding shelter and moorage at numerous bays throughout the islands.

Mayne Island

While the wilderness is wonderful, Mayne Island offers a wholesome portion of history as well. Native tribes inhabited Helen Point 5,000 years ago.

Evidence remains in the middens and white beaches formed from eroded clam, abalone and oyster shells. In the late 1850s, rowdy miners stopped here en route from Victoria to the gold-fields of Barkerville; some returned to enjoy the relatively mild winters. At the turn of the last century, British gentry liked to spend their summers on Mayne.

The lighthouse at Georgina Point, built in 1855, still guides vessels into the eastern entrance to Active Pass. The lighthouse is open to visitors every day from 1pm to 3pm (no admission charge).

The best-loved country church on Mayne Island is St Mary Magdalene's, built in 1898 on a hill overlooking Active Pass. The 180-kg (397-pound) sandstone font was carried by rowing boat from Saturna Island in 1900.

The Mayne Island Gaol is open in summer (no admission charge). Built in 1896, it is now a museum housing memorabilia from the 19th century, including remnants from the sailing barque *Zephyr* which hit the Georgina shoals and sank in 1872. Check out *www.mayneislandchamber.ca*

Galiano Island

Coon Bay, Bluff Park, Mt Sutil and Mt Galiano have fine views. Montague Provincial Park offers wildlife (*for more information see www.galianoisland.com*).

Pender Islands

Famous for beaches and coves, and the Driftwood Centre and craft shops at Port Washington, as well as wildlife. *Events: Salmon BBQ and Fish Derby* *(July); Art Show, Fall Fair (Aug).* *www.penderisland.info*

Saltspring Island

Look out for art and craft galleries, village shops and the Saturday-morning market at Ganges. Views at Mt Maxwell and Ruckle Provincial Park are superb. *Events: Round the Island Race (May); Sea Capers (June); Art/Craft Exhibition (June–Sept); Fall Fair (Sept).* *www.saltspringisland.org*

Saturna Island

East Point Lighthouse. Lyall Harbour pub and store. Winter Cove Marine Park. Wildlife, including ravens and wild goats. *Events: Lamb Barbecue (July).* *www.saturnatourism.com*

For more information on the Gulf Islands, contact Tourism Association of Vancouver Island, *203–335 Wesley St, Nanaimo. Tel: (250) 754 3500. Also see www.gulfislands.net*

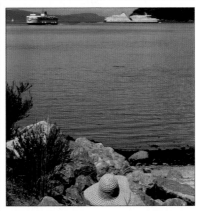

Wonderful views over the sea can be had from various vantage points on Mayne Island

HAIDA GWAII
(QUEEN CHARLOTTE ISLANDS)

The Charlottes, named Haida Gwaii by the native Haida people, comprise two main islands, **Graham** and **Moresby**, and 150 little ones, together covering an area of 9,000sq km (3,475sq miles). They lie north of Vancouver Island and about 120km (75 miles) west of Prince Rupert (*see map on pp22–3*). Frequently hidden under a grey blanket of cloud and fog, Haida Gwaii is surrounded by treacherous seas and rocks. The Cape St James weather station, hugging the southern tip of the southernmost island, is the windiest one in Canada. But it is also the warmest, thanks to soothing Kuroshio currents crossing the Pacific Ocean from Japan.

Much of empty Moresby Island is parkland, a result of efforts by Haida and other environmentalists. Although fishermen by tradition, the 2,000 Haida who live here today are celebrated for beautifully carved wooden masks, canoes, totem poles, and smaller items shaped in argillite, an ebony slate mudstone. A few hundred years ago, about 8,000 Haida lived here, famed in the region as fierce warriors. But they were decimated by Caucasian diseases, probably beginning in 1774, when the first European, Juan José Pérez, sailed round the northern coast.

Grey, weathered totem poles still stand at several abandoned villages throughout these rugged isles. The most accessible is Yan, in the north of Graham Island. A visiting permit can be purchased from the local chief, who can arrange boats and guides. The Haida, who claim 10,000 years of experience,

Haida craftsman at work

also organise tours to the South Moresby National Park and Ninstints (**Anthony Island**), site of the largest cluster of original standing totem poles in the world.

Although about 6,000 people in all now live in Haida Gwaii, there are no banks or shopping malls. The isolation and the mists have, over the years, attracted many interesting characters, some who came to the islands because they were different, and others who became different because they came to the islands.

The moss-draped forests of the Galapagos North, as Haida Gwaii is sometimes called, provide a dreamy silence for the shy black-tailed deer, Roosevelt elk and black bear that live in them. On the eastern shores, where the murmuring sea washes broad crescents of pebbles and sand, loons call soulfully over the waters and bald eagles squeal overhead from shadowing stands of ancient cedar and Sitka spruce. Whales, sea lions, porpoises and puffins live offshore. Anglers usually go home with catches of rock and ling cod, salmon,

halibut, trout and red snapper. Fishing remains a strong industry, but logging is fast disappearing.
For more information see www.haidagwaii.ca

Delkatla Wildlife Sanctuary

This park is of special interest to birdwatchers because of the more than 100 native and migrating species of birds that have been spotted here, including auklets, petrels, puffins and sandhill cranes.
On a salt marsh near Masset, Graham Island. Tel: (250) 626 5015; www.birdsanctuary.org. Open: daily.

Naikoon Provincial Park

Naikoon (means 'rose point' in Haida) Park, set in 72,640 hectares (179,497 acres), offers 100km (62 miles) of beaches. It contains many hiking trails, including one to Tow Hill, which overlooks an agate beach and an unusual lava formation. Sitka deer and the rare Peale's peregrine falcon can be spotted here.
On the east coast between Tlell and Masset, Graham Island. Tel: (250) 557 4390. Open: daily.

Queen Charlotte Islands Museum

The museum has argillite carvings, cedar totem poles, natural history exhibits and relics of the early

European settlements. The longhouse shelters several canoes, including Loo-Taas (Wave-eater), designed by master carver Bill Reid.
Second Beach Rd, Skidegate, Graham Island. Tel: (250) 559 4643. Open: Tue–Sun 9am–4pm (summer); afternoons only (winter). Admission charge. For more information contact the Northern BC Tourism Association (tel: (250) 561 0432, toll free (800) 663 8843).

How to get there

Air Canada (*tel: 1 888 247 2262; www.aircanada.com*) jets twice daily from Vancouver to Sandspit on northeast Moresby Island. You can also fly from Prince Rupert with Harbour Air to Sandspit on Moresby Island. Car rental is expensive and getting around the islands is difficult. BC Ferries (*tel: 1 888 BCFERRY or (604) 386 3431*) make the 6-hour run from Prince Rupert to Skidegate every day in summer, and three times weekly in winter. A 20-minute ferry runs every hour or two between Moresby Island and Graham Island, where most of the relatively small choice of motels and hotels are located.

A rugged Haida Gwaii beach

QUADRA ISLAND

Quadra Island lies off Vancouver Island's northeast coast, just a 10-minute ferry ride across Discovery Passage from the salmon-fishing centre of Campbell River.

In addition to native Indian culture and regional cuisine, the island offers many options for outdoor recreation, including kayaking, canoeing, scuba diving, whale watching and fishing.

Landlubbers can enjoy beachcombing at Rebecca Spit, hiking the trails or climbing up Chinese Mountain for the spectacular view, and mountain biking.

For history buffs, there are interesting ruins to explore at the Lucky Jim Mine, and ancient Indian petroglyphs or stone drawings at Francisco Point, We-wai-kai Beach and Cape Mudge.

Kwakiutl Museum

This snail-shaped structure shelters about 300 items confiscated by the Canadian government in 1922 when it outlawed the *potlatch*, a ceremonial celebration where one tribe hosts another and showers it with gifts.

The displays include headdresses, masks, woven cedar baskets, bent boxes, a three-storey-high totem pole and a collection of early 20th-century photos.
37 Weway Rd, Cape Mudge. Tel: (250) 285 3733. Open: Tue–Sat 10am–4.30pm; shorter hours in winter.
Admission charge.

How to get there
There are regular scheduled flights from Vancouver Airport to Campbell River, and a daily floatplane service from Coal Harbour to Campbell River.

Vancouver's islands

Carpenter Lake
Bralonne
Lake Seton
Lillooet
Cache Creek
Ashcroft
Toba
Toba
Mountains
Lillooet
Birkenhead Lake Prov. Park
Anderson Lake
D'Arcy
Birken
▲ Blustery Mt 2329 m
Thompson
Squamish
Pemberton
■ Joffre Lakes
Spences Bridge
lation Sound Marine Park
Mount Currie
Lillooet Lake
▲ Skihist Mt 2944 m
Lytton
ell e
Whistler
Wedge Mt 2891 m ▲
Keefers
Jervis Inlet
▲ Mt Churchill 2003 m
Whistler/Blackcomb Ski Area
Garibaldi
Garibaldi Provincial Park
Lillooet Range
Boston Bar
Cheakamus
ery Bay
Jervis Inlet
Egmont
Earls Cove
Sunshine Coast
Lake Lovely Water Recreation Area
▲ Mt Garibaldi 2678 m
Spuzzum
Fraser
Halfmoon Bay
Porteau Cove
Porpoise Bay
■ Squamish
Golden Ears Provincial Park
Yale
Sechelt
Britannia Beach
Howe Sound
Pitt
Roberts Creek
Langdale
Lion's Bay
Mt Seymour Prov Park
Harrison Lake
Sasquatch Park
Gibsons
Pitt Lake
Hope
trevor h Park
Georgia
Horseshoe Bay
North Vancouver
Stave Lake
noose Bay
Nanaimo
Gabriola Island
VANCOUVER
Port Moody
Harrison Hot Springs
Skagit Valley Prov Rec Area
Manning Provincial Park
Richmond ■
New Westminster
Mission ■
Minter Gardens
Valdes Island
Matsqui
Chilliwack
oglyph Park
Ladysmith
Tsawwassen
White Rock
Peach Arch ■ Park
Abbotsford
Chilliwack Lake
u
Galiano Island
■ Cultus Lake Park
Lake Cowichan
Chemainus
Active Pass
Mayne Island
Saltspring Island
North Pender I
Saturna Island
Duncan
South Pender I
Gulf Islands
Bellingham
North Cascades National Park
Swartz Bay
Sidney
Butchart Gardens ■
Saanich
WASHINGTON
Sooke
Victoria
Mount Vernon
USA
Strait
Port Angeles
Puget Sound
Olympic National Park
Everett

0   20   40   60   80km

0   10   20   30   40   50 miles

VANCOUVER ISLAND

Islands conjure up all kinds of images, and Vancouver Island is no exception. Stretching 450km (280 miles) along Canada's Pacific coast, this huge island brings to mind images of mossy, dense and dark rainforests of fir, cedar and hemlock; barren, wind- and surf-swept Pacific beaches; Edwardian lampposts draped with baskets of trailing flowers; and elegant Victorian afternoon teas.

Victoria

BC is no longer predominantly British, as more and more people from different cultures and countries around the world continue to move here to live. But Victoria, the provincial capital, which began as a Hudson's Bay trading post in 1843, still retains some elements of British life – traditional afternoon tea,

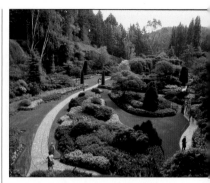

The Butchart Gardens, north of Victoria, are a showcase of floral displays

Victoria

and a sense of propriety and order. Victorians, like many island people, tend to be more relaxed and forgiving. Perhaps this is because the sun shines more than in Vancouver, a mere 100km north.

With its historic buildings, colourful old Chinatown, museums and lovely parks and gardens, Victoria offers visitors much to see and do. But for a different day, call Victoria Carriage Tours (*tel: (250) 383 2207, toll free (877) 663 2207; www.victoriacarriage.com*), and ride around the city in a classic vintage carriage drawn by a single white horse.

Alternatively, take a harbour cruise, go fishing, or splash away a summer day at the All Fun Waterslides on Millstream Road, a 15-minute drive from the city centre (*tel: (250) 474 3184; open: only in the summer*).

Butchart Gardens

Possibly the most spectacular floral display on the continent today, these gardens began as an abandoned limestone quarry in 1904. Meandering paved pathways lead through 20 hectares (49 acres) of exquisite arrangements of more than 5,000 varieties of trees, shrubs and flowers. There is a sunken garden, rose garden, Japanese garden, Italian garden, star pond, concert lawn, fireworks basin, show greenhouse, seed store, two restaurants and a coffee bar.

In summer, additional entertainment includes musical reviews, puppet shows, night illuminations and fireworks, while in winter, after the kaleidoscope of colourful blossoms has faded, ribbons of lights brighten the grey days. Wheelchairs, cameras, baby pushcarts and umbrellas are available for hire. *800 Benvenuto Ave, about 21km (13 miles) north of Victoria via Highway 17 and Keating Cross Rd. Tel: toll free 1 866 652 4422; www.butchartgardens.com. Open: daily 9am. Closing times vary – call or visit website.*

Helmcken House
The oldest house in BC open to the public was built in 1842. It provides a glimpse into the life of a pioneer physician 150 years ago. The house has become part of the Royal BC Museum. *251 Superior St. For more information, contact the Royal BC Museum, tel: (250) 356 7226, toll free (888) 447 7077.*

The Legislature
Hourly guided tours show off this stately greystone structure and its intricate stained-glass windows, Italian marble panels, mosaic tile floors and painted murals illustrating the farming, fishing, mining and logging past of the province.

On the Inner Harbour. Tel: (250) 387 3046; www.parl-bldgs.gov.bc.ca. Open: Mon–Fri 9am–5pm; summer weekends (May–Sept) 9am–5pm.

Royal BC Museum
The Royal BC Museum rates in many people's eyes as the finest museum in Canada, with displays of BC history which include a woolly mammoth, cobblestone streets bordered by Victorian storefronts, a working gold-rush waterwheel, a replica of Captain George Vancouver's ship *Discovery* and the magical masks and totem poles of the First Nations. *675 Belleville St. Tel: (250) 356 7226; www.royalbcmuseum.bc.ca. Open: daily 9am–5pm. Admission charge.*

Thunderbird Park
This downtown park has an outdoor display of replicas of old totem poles and original contemporary poles, and carvings by coastal Indian artists. *Beside Helmcken House.*

For information on other attractions and activities, visit the *Travel InfoCentre* which is situated at *812 Wharf St. Tel: (250) 382 2127; www.tourismvictoria.com*

Victoria harbour

North to Nanaimo
'The Little Town That Did'

An hour's drive north from Victoria on the Malahat Highway (Highway 1) is the little coastal town of **Chemainus**. In the early 1980s, when the century-old sawmill closed and the town lay dying, a few artists began drawing larger-than-life murals on the exterior walls of buildings. Today, the town boasts Canada's largest outdoor art gallery, with 36 murals depicting the history of the Chemainus Valley. Subjects range from a 19th-century brigantine to Hong Hing's grocery store and portraits of First Nations people.

The town also has antique shops, art galleries, boutiques selling local crafts and souvenirs, and ice-cream parlours. A friendly place for lunch is The Willow St Cafe, lodged in a 100-year-old heritage building. Try some quesadillas or daily special lunches on the spacious outdoor patio (*tel: (250) 246 2434. Open daily 9am–5pm*). The annual Festival of Murals in July and August is a lively affair; you can see painters and sculptors at work, puppeteers, dramatists, street dances and parades.

Wayside diversions

Three kilometres south of Nanaimo, right beside the road from Victoria, is tiny **Petroglyph Park**. If you blink, you might miss it. A short stroll through the woods leads to a series of ancient Indian rock carvings depicting people, birds, bottomfish and the mythical seawolf.

'The Harbour City'

Nanaimo is best known as the 'Bathtub Capital of the World', referring to the annual mid-July festival when dozens of tubbers challenge the often choppy waters to race 54km (34 miles) across Georgia Strait to Kitsilano Beach in Vancouver (*www. bathtub.island.net*). Also called 'The Harbour City', Nanaimo is a key link in the BC Ferries chain, with frequent regular sailings to and from Tsawwassen and Horseshoe Bay on the Lower Mainland.

A walking tour of the old town should include the Nanaimo District Museum, 100 Cameron Street (*tel: (250) 753 1821*), which has exhibits

SNORKELLING WITH SALMON

If any life form can be called totemic for British Columbia, it's the salmon. For centuries, the many species (coho, steelhead, chum, Chinook, pink and sockeye) formed the basis of the First Nations diet and inspired their art. Today its popularity continues not only as a delicious food and for sports fishing, but also as one of BC's newest adventures – snorkelling with salmon. A company called Paradise Found in Campbell River provides wet suits, guides and all the necessary snorkelling gear. Peeking at the fish in deep eddies, running the rapids or simply floating along with schools of salmon all around is a true adrenaline high.

Paradise Found Adventure Tours. *Tel: (250) 923 0848; info@paradisefound.bc.ca; www.paradisefound.bc.ca*

explaining such events as the arrival of the Spanish, and discovery of coal, as well as artefacts of Vancouver Island's native peoples. The highlight of the area is The Bastion, on Front Street, built by the Hudson Bay Company in 1853 to protect settlers from attack. Today it serves as a landmark and is guarded by two of its original cannons.

Nanaimo is also famous for its chocolate bars called Nanaimo Bars. The bars comprise butter, icing sugar, a mixture of graham crackers and coconut, wrapped in rich layers of chocolate.

Although several typical restaurants such as The Blue Ginger (*5769 Turner Rd; tel: (250) 751 8238*) and the Lighthouse Bistro (*50 Anchor Way; tel: (250) 754 3212*) specialise in local seafood, the Mexican food at Gina's (*tel: (250) 753 5411*) is more fun. Perched on a clifftop across from the law courts, this cosy little restaurant is friendly, prices are reasonable, the clientele interesting and the sunset views superb. Nanaimo claims more retail space per head than any other place in North America, so shoppers can have lots of fun.

Spot the real people standing in front of a colourful mural at Chemainus!

Both ornithologists and amateur naturalists love BC birdwatching, one of the fastest-growing recreational activities in the province. BC is home to some 400 species of birds, representing more than 80 per cent of all the species found in Canada. Birds are not only much less elusive than other wild creatures in BC, but also offer cheery songs without discrimination to both downtown city dwellers and adventurers on remote mountain trails.

The easily accessible Lower Mainland region is home to numerous species of birds, while others winter here to escape the northern Arctic winds and snows, and still others stop to feed and rest during annual migrations.

In Vancouver, some elderly West End residents make a weekly ritual of greeting and feeding the ducks and swans around Lost Lagoon, on the fringe of Stanley Park. Park traffic sometimes stops to allow a gaggle of Canada geese to cross the road. At the rocky cliffs near Siwash Rock, cormorants, gulls and guillemots make their nests, and within the forest bald eagles can be seen perched on tall trees.

Kingfishers and great blue herons are often seen hunting at Coal Harbour, Vancouver Island, along with loons, whose lonesome yodel symbolises the solitude of the Canadian wilderness.

Iona Island, in Richmond, is a good place to observe grebes, ducks, hawks, owls and passerines, while Pitt Meadows, in the Fraser Valley, is home to green herons, ducks, sandhill cranes, hawks and owls. But the best place for birdwatching is probably the **Reifel Bird Sanctuary**, located on the swampy, salty delta of the Fraser River. This area is home to Canada's largest concentration of waterfowl, including about 40,000 snow geese. The birds are best seen here from September to May.

Bird Alert (*tel: (250) 592 3381*) provides details of rare and unusual birds sighted in the Greater Vancouver area.

The rich and diverse opportunities for birdwatching in BC are a delight for expert ornithologists and amateur birdwatchers alike

Safe paddling at Parksville

Parksville

Nowhere in Canada does the ocean wash the shoreline so gently as it does along the popular sunny and sheltered bay at Parksville, the hub of Vancouver Island's east-coast 'Beach Country'. Today, about 45,000 people live in the triangle formed by Parksville and nearby Qualicum Beach and Coombs.

When Captain Vancouver explored the area two centuries ago, only Coast Salish Indians were living here. First settled in 1870, Parksville prospered steadily for many years with an economy based on forestry, tourism and farming. But in recent years development has been more spectacular, with large numbers of Canadians moving in to settle and to spend holidays enjoying the area's special attractions.

Beaches and sandcastles

The waters of the Strait of Georgia flow in regularly twice a day along this coast. But whether the tide is in or out, there is ample space on the beach for a family outing or a solitary stroll.

Low tide leaves great expanses of hard, clean sand several hundred metres wide. This is the time when beach-combers come to hunt for oysters and dig for clams, local residents walk their dogs, and visitors and their children wade in the shallow pools, fly kites and build sandcastles.

The week-long Sandcastle Contest every August attracts master builders from around the world, and they have to work quickly to complete their creations in the damp sand while the tide is out. Another competition is held specially for the children (*tel: (250) 248 3613*).

At high tide, the hot summer sand warms the incoming water to a comfortable swimming temperature. Parksville beach claims the warmest outdoor swimming conditions in the province, with summer temperatures averaging 21°C (70°F). The shallow water provides an ideal waterpark where youngsters may safely swim, splash about, and ride dinghies and tubes.

The beach is probably at its most memorable in the early morning, when the loons are calling, the seals are barking and, across the water, the distant, deep mauve mountains are emerging against the orange sky.

South of Parksville, more than 2km of sandy shore also beckon at **Rathtrevor Beach Provincial Park** (for reservations, call *(604) 689 2025*), one of the most popular family camping spots on Vancouver Island.

There are also 4km (2^1/$_2$ miles) of hiking trails frequented by deer and rabbits, dozens of picnic tables and barbecue pits, children's play areas, a nature house, an amphitheatre and, in summer, nature interpretative programmes.

Special area attractions

As a change from the beach, Paradise Adventure Golf (*tel: (250) 248 6612*), centrally located in Parksville, also offers fun for the whole family. The two 18-hole miniature courses have a fantasy setting, with a pirate galleon, Victorian mansion, watermill, lighthouse and bright floral displays.

For history lovers, **Craig Heritage Park and Museum** (*tel: (250) 248 6966*), 3km (2 miles) south of town, recalls the past with the 1912 Knox Church, the century-old French Creek post office, the McMillan loghouse, the Montrose school, a World War II fire station, and collections of late 19th-century clothing, old logging and farming equipment and early photographs of the area.

The Parksville coast is a birdwatchers' paradise, with its abundance of bald eagles, blue herons, loons, harlequin ducks and trumpeter swans.

Of the 57 species found here, 19 are on the North American birdwatchers' list of most keenly sought birds. One of these is the Brent goose, about 20,000 of which stop here during March and April to feed on the Pacific herring which spawns offshore, on the way to their Alaska nesting grounds. The event is celebrated every April during Parksville's Brant Wildlife Festival (*tel: (250) 752 9171; www.brantfestival.bc.ca*). The area is also a haven for anglers who come from far and wide to fish the waters.

Places to eat and stay

Accommodation for visitors in the Parksville-Qualicum Beach-Coombs area includes 1,500 hotel and motel units ranging from rustic cabins to modern condominiums and luxury beach resorts, with an additional 2,000 camping and recreational vehicle (RV) sites.

A range of fast-food and family eating places can be found along the Island Highway. There are also more elegant gourmet restaurants, including the picturesque historic MacLure House (*1015, East Island Highway; tel: (250) 248 3470; www.maclurehouse.com*), once a private, Scottish-style manor house and now partly used as a small guesthouse.

For further information on the Parksville-Qualicum Beach-Coombs area, contact the Parksville & District Chamber of Commerce, *PO Box 99, Parksville, BC V9P 2G3*, or visit: *www.chamber.parksville.bc.ca*
The tourism information office is about 3km (2 miles) south of Parksville (*tel: (250) 248 3613*).

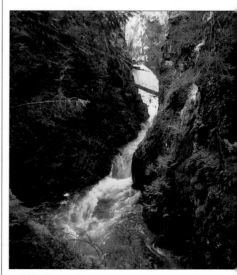

Little Qualicum Falls

Qualicum Beach

Qualicum Beach
(*www.qualicum.bc.ca*) is a
mecca for outdoor lovers
and fishing enthusiasts.
The Old School House
(*tel: (250) 752 6133;
www.theoldschoolhouse.org*),
affectionately known as
TOSH, is about 80 years
old. It was renovated in the
mid-1980s to house an art
gallery with changing
exhibits and eight studios
with big viewing windows,
so that visitors can watch
resident artists at work.

Another interesting
building, the Qualicum
Heritage Inn, is housed in a
former boarding school and
sits on 2 hectares (5 acres)
overlooking the ocean
(*tel: (250) 752 9292; www.
qualicumheritageinn.com*).

Numerous companies
scattered along the coast
offer charters of both
powerboats and sailing
boats, large and small.
Travellers should contact
the Parksville/Qualicum
Beach Tourism Association
(*tel: (250) 248 3613; www.
chamber.parksville.bc.ca or
www.tourismmall.victoria.
bc.ca/aavanisle/pqboats*).

Anglers flock to this area
for the fighting coho,
halibut and cod in the
saltchuck around several
offshore islands, and for
the trout and steelhead in
mountain streams and in
the Big Qualicum, Little
Qualicum and Englishman
rivers.

Good golf courses in the
neighbourhood include the
Fairwinds (18 holes; *tel:
(250) 468 7666*) on the
Nanoose Peninsula, the
Eaglecrest (18 holes; *tel:
(250) 752 6311*) just south
of Qualicum Beach, the
Qualicum Beach Memorial
(9 holes; *tel: (250) 752
6312*) on Crescent Road,
and the Morningstar (18
holes; *tel: (250) 248 8161;
www.golfvancouverisland.
ca*) near the French Creek
Marina.

Coombs

A 10-minute drive inland
from Qualicum Beach,
following Highway 4 to
Port Alberni and Long
Beach, is the tiny town of
Coombs, instantly
identifiable in summer by
the goats grazing on the
grass roof of the roadside
Old Country Market. The
surrounding cluster of
shops sells everything from
candied apples and antler
carvings to sportswear. The
Bluegrass Festival and Old
Time Fiddlers' Contest
held every summer attract
country-and-western fans
from all over the continent

CATHEDRAL GROVE

About halfway along
Highway 4, between
Parksville and Port Alberni,
stands Cathedral Grove,
in McMillan Park. Well-
marked wilderness trails,
carpeted with coniferous
needles and cedar chips,
meander through lush
ferns, hemlocks, cedars
and a grove of 800-year-
old Douglas fir trees,
which survived a forest fire
300 years ago. The largest
tree measures 3m (10 feet)
in diameter and 9m
(30 feet) in circumference,
and stands 75m (246 feet)
tall. Interpretative signs
explain the woodland
cycle of growth and decay.
Little wonder this is called
Cathedral Grove, for the
elegant, moss-draped trees
create a sanctuary as awe-
inspiring as any ancient
religious building in
Europe.

– probably a far cry from the demure, God-fearing colony intended when Salvation Army Commissioner Coombs led a dozen English families here to settle in 1910.

Nearby **Butterfly World** (Highway 4A; *tel: (250) 248 7026*) houses hundreds of exotic butterflies, representing 70 species, flying free in an enclosed tropical garden. Visitors can watch butterflies emerging from cocoons, flying, courting, sipping nectar, laying eggs or simply basking in the sunlight. Be sure to brush any butterflies off your shoulders before you leave.

A few kilometres further along the highway westward, Hillier's Sausage Factory (*tel: (250) 752 2390*) is an essential stop for campers and almost anyone else, since the European-style smoked meats made here are among the best in Canada.

Two provincial parks where outdoor lovers can walk, fish, swim, picnic or camp are also accessible from Coombs via Highway 4.

East of town, and some 16km south of the highway, is **Englishman River Falls Park**, with its impressive waterfall, gorges and pools set in forests of cedar, hemlock and fir trees.

Further west, on the way to Port Alberni, is **Little Qualicum Falls** with superb cataracts, pools and rocky chasms below Cameron Lake.

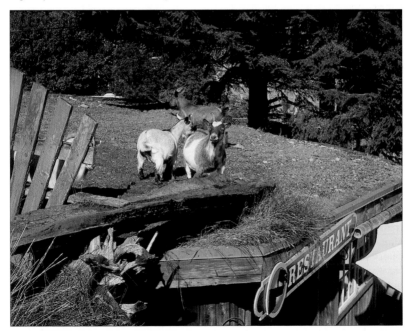

Coombs market with resident 'roof goats'

Port Alberni

Port Alberni, a town of some 20,000 people, is the gateway to Vancouver Island's spectacular west coast and Pacific Rim National Park. About a three-hour drive from Victoria, it lies at the head of the long saltwater Alberni Inlet, midway along scenic Highway 4, which crosses the island's rugged interior. Named after the Spanish explorer Pedro Alberni, who passed through the area two centuries ago, the town sprawls around the lumber yards and mills of the MacMillan Bloedel timber company.

As the 'Salmon Capital of the World', Port Alberni is also a major fishing port, landing 20 per cent of BC's annual salmon catch from the 300 commercial fishing boats operating out of its harbour. Keen anglers flock here year-round to fish the salmon-rich waters of Alberni Inlet and nearby Barkley Sound. The most experienced especially enjoy Labour Day weekend here, when they compete in contests for more than $50,000 in prizes during the annual Clutesi Salmon Festival (Clutesi Haven Marina; *tel: (250) 724 6837*).

These competitions draw crowds to Alberni Harbour Quay, where the Clock Tower provides a panoramic view for miles around. Apart from the gift shops, art galleries, restaurants and boat companies offering cruises and fishing charters, the lively quayside offers live outdoor entertainment and rides on the little 'Two Spot' steam engine (*June–Sept*). The Quay is a great spot for visitors to mix and mingle, sample a meal or two, find a souvenir or watch

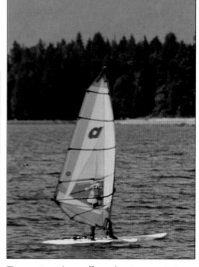

The great outdoors offers adventure sports to suit all tastes

the locals while sipping a drink at one of the outdoor cafés.

Port Alberni is a good base for various outdoor activities in the area. Nearby Mount Arrowsmith (1,800m/5,906 feet), which is snowcapped for most of the year, has a number of forest trails which are suitable for hiking in summer or skiing in winter. A half-hour drive south of town along a rough logging road is China Creek, a popular spot for windsurfers where skill-testing regattas are held every summer.
(*For more information see: www.city.port-alberni.bc.ca*)

Sproat Lake

Only a 15-minute drive west out of Port Alberni via Highway 4, the community of Sproat Lake borders the vast freshwater lake and provincial park of the same name. This is the home base of the Martin Mars water-bombers, the largest firefighting aircraft in the world, with tail-wing tips standing almost five storeys high. As they take off, these mammoth planes scoop up water from the lake to douse forest fires. Visitors are sometimes admitted to their land base, about a 10-minute walk east from the rustic Maples Resort on the north shore. But the planes are perhaps best seen from the deck of the Fish and Duck pub (*tel: (250) 724 4331*) as they become silhouettes against the setting sun.

One of the most dramatic rainforest walks in the world is the short and little-known, but marked, trail from the water-bomber base to Sproat Lake Park. From the campsites, picnic tables and boat-launching ramp in the park, it is another 10-minute walk east along the lakeshore to a floating dock from which some of the most interesting ancient petroglyphs on Vancouver Island can be viewed.

North of Sproat Lake, another intriguing place to visit is the **Robertson** **Creek Hatchery** (*tel: (250) 724 6521;* open: daily 8am–4pm) on the Stamp River, where millions of chinook, coho and steelhead are bred annually. Tours are available year-round, but the best time to visit is in September or October. During these months, the mature salmon return upstream after four years at sea and leap up a series of fish ladders in Stamp Falls Provincial Park (*tel: (250) 954 4600*) to spawn at their birthplace.

Sproat Lake is also a good jumping-off point for an exciting two- to four-day excursion that includes a canoe or water-taxi ride along the entire length of nearby **Great Central Lake**, followed by a 16-km (10-mile) hike along a trail to the spectacular **Della Falls**. Plunging 444m (1,457 feet) in three magnificent cascades, the falls are among the highest in Canada.

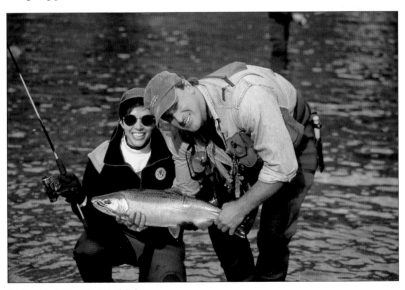

A big catch is every angler's delight

Lady Rose

Gracious but hardworking, the MV *Lady Rose* (*tel: (250) 723 8313; www.ladyrosemarine.com*) is a sturdy 32-m (105-foot) long diesel packet, built in Glasgow in 1937, and has been ferrying freight and passengers for over half a century. She is licensed to carry 100 passengers, and now offers visitors memorable sailing adventures. The MV *Frances Barkley* is a newer sister ship and takes over some of the destinations such as the Broken Island Group.

At 8am, a shrill blast announces departure from the Port Alberni quay for the voyage westward down Alberni Inlet to the Pacific Ocean. Passengers take breakfast or settle comfortably on the deck to enjoy the scenery. Dark forests rise sharply from the edges of the broad fiord. The ship sails along at a steady 12 knots past China Creek and then ties up at the floating post office dock in Kildonan to unload mail and crates of goods. The next stops are at a couple of commercial fish farms, where groceries and pallets of fish food are delivered. Bald eagles circle overhead, hoping for left-overs. Then the *Lady Rose* sails on to several isolated logging camps to unload mail and machinery parts.

In the summer, (*June–Sept*), the *Frances Barkley* now takes visitors further north to the **Broken Islands Group**,

IF YOU GO

Pack sunscreen lotion, a warm sweater, a raincoat or windcheater, and wear sensible shoes. The weather in Alberni Inlet may vary from hot sunshine to heavy rain and strong winds. Bring a camera and binoculars for watching birds and possibly seals and grey whales. Canoes and single and double kayaks, to enjoy the raw natural beauty of the Broken Islands, can be hired on a daily or weekly basis.

Remember that the ships are working vessels, so dress accordingly. For reservations and further information, call toll free *1 800 663 7192* from April to September; the rest of the year call *(250) 723 8313*.

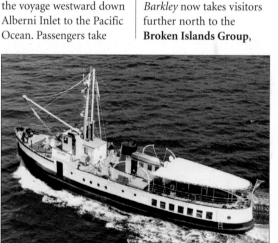

A famous lady – *Lady Rose*

in Barkley Sound. This cluster of about 100 small islands has several sheltered lagoons filled with sea birds and marine life that attract canoeists, kayakers and scuba divers. By noon the ship is docking at West Bamfield, where wooden boardwalks meander along the waterfront. As there is no road access here, water taxis cross the cove to East Bamfield, which is connected by a rough gravel logging road to Port Alberni. Accommodation is available for an overnight stay. Otherwise, the stopover time here may be from 40 minutes to 1½ hours.

The *Frances Barkley* also travels through the Broken Islands Group, stopping at the Sechart Whaling Station, to drop off and pick up wilderness lovers laden with backpacks and other sporting equipment. She then stops for about an

Sailing adventures await along the waterfront

hour at the fishing village of Ucluelet, before heading back up Alberni Inlet. The arrival back at Port Alberni is usually between 5.30pm and 6.30pm.

The *Frances Barkley* carries backpackers looking to get away from it all

BC's lumber industry

The Pacific Northwest rainforests, among the most luxuriant in the world, contain trees more than 1,000 years old. More than half of BC is covered in forest, most of it on Crown land. To protect the resources for the future, a Forest Practices Code was established in June 1995.

The government grants tree-farming licences to logging companies, who are supposed to take care of the forest, clean up any waste and plant new trees. A dozen companies control more than 80 per cent of the provincial timber resources, and more than 90 per cent of the pulp mills and plywood plants. Until the 1980s, only about one-third of the cleared land was being reforested. Fortunately that is now changing, as more people are becoming increasingly aware of the necessity of preserving natural resources. Public protests are forcing forestry companies to take better care of the forests, with selective cutting and more planting.

The traditional lumberjack, in his long-sleeved checked shirt and heavy boots, has disappeared. The axe has been replaced by chainsaws, bulldozers, tree stumpers, hydraulic barkers, loaders, sorters and other machinery. In addition to loggers, the industry employs heavy-equipment operators, truck drivers, sawmill, pulp and paper-plant workers and tugboat captains.

After the chainsaws fell the trees, the branches are removed, and cranes move the logs to the roadside, where loading machines stack the logs onto trucks. The logs are then carried to a dumping ground and are sorted, measured and bundled. The biggest and best logs, such as the strong Douglas fir, go to plywood and other sawmills. Such smaller logs as western hemlock and balsam fir go to pulp and paper mills. Western red cedar, which is both weather- and rot-resistant, is often used for making roofing shales and shingles.

BC's luxuriant forests are a major economic resource for the province and for Canada

Pacific Rim National Park Reserve

No trip to Vancouver Island is complete without a visit to the wild and rugged Pacific Rim National Park Reserve on the western side of the island. Annual rainfall here averages 300cm (118 inches), so before setting out check *www.theweathernetwork.com/features/parks* or call (250) 726 7721 for the weather forecast. The park is divided into three areas: from north to south, Long Beach, the Broken Islands Group and the West Coast Trail. More details at: *www.parkscan.harbour.com/pacrim*

Long Beach

Long Beach is accessible by car along a winding mountain highway from Port Alberni. Solitary walkers love this broad 11-km (7-mile) long stretch of surf-swept sand, rocky outcrops and tidal pools. Big drift-logs, bull kelp and brilliant sea anemones and starfish dot the sands, where lucky beachcombers can occasionally pick up glass fishing floats, watermarked like sterling silver to identify the villages in Japan from where they came. When summer surf is up at Incinerator Rock, it is fun to watch surfers catching the waves ashore.

The **Wickaninnish Centre** (*tel: (250) 726 7706*) lends insight to the sometimes harsh haven that is the blue Pacific. Exhibits, murals, audio-visual presentations and other interpretative programmes explain the natural and human history of the region. The restaurant here is a good spot to admire the coast.

The two towns nearby, **Ucluelet** and **Tofino**, offer a variety of restaurants and accommodation. Tofino, surrounded by water on three sides, has several craft shops and art galleries. The Blue Heron (*tel: (250) 725 3277*) serves good seafood in an informal setting, and the Pacific Sands Beach Resort (*tel: (250) 725 3322, toll free (800) 565 BEACH; www.pacificsands.com*) has 60 rooms with balconies overlooking Cox Bay.

The West Coast Trail

Hardy hikers love the West Coast Trail, which meanders for 77km (48 miles) along an old telegraph route through

WHALE WATCHING

Every spring from mid-March to mid-April, Pacific Rim National Park becomes a popular place for whale watching.

As their northbound migration reaches its peak, the 15-m (49-foot) long grey whales swim close to shore, often pausing to play in the coves and inlets along the coast.

Although whales are frequently sighted from rocky headlands along Long Beach, charter boat companies, such as **Jamie's Whaling Station** in Tofino (*tel: (250) 725 3919, toll free (800) 667 9913; www.jamies.com*) and **Remote Passages** (*tel: (250) 725 3330, toll free (800) 666 9833; www.remotepassages.com*), organise excursions.

The **Pacific Rim Whale Festival** at Tofino and Ucluelet (*tel: (250) 726 7798*) includes crab races, a gumboot golf tournament, concerts and plays.

The 'Whales in the Park' programmes include free guided whale-spotting hikes, lectures and films.

wilderness rainforest, along sandstone cliffs and across slippery boardwalks in the southern part of **Pacific Rim National Park**. This rugged coastline was known as the graveyard of the Pacific for all the ships which sank off its shores.

The hike, which takes about a week to complete, is not for the faint-hearted. About a quarter of the hikers who set out do not manage to finish. But the challengers of this treacherous trail, accessible from mid-May to September only, are rewarded with the smell of the salty sea air; breathtaking views of undisturbed shoreline; occasional sightings of pods of whales and pudgy sea lions, and such sea birds as pigeon guillemots, marbled murrelets and pelagic cormorants; such treasures as Tsusiat Falls, where several cascades have created super swimming holes near the shore; and a campfire under the stars.

The trail runs from Port Renfrew (*tel: (250) 647 5434*) to Bamfield (*tel: (250) 728 3234*), or vice versa. To reserve, *tel: (250) 387 1642 or (604) 435 5622, or toll free 1 800-HELLO BC; www.hellobc.com. Park open: summer only; reservations required.*

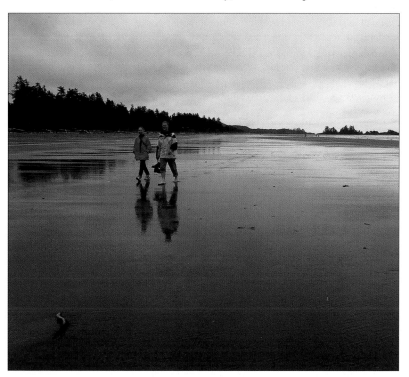

Storms at Chesterman Beach, Tofino

Tour: Sunshine Circle

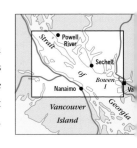

Travellers trying to cram a lot into a two-week holiday in BC coastal country find a circular tour makes sense. This driving circuit includes four ferry rides (queues can be horrendous in summer) and covers the Sunshine Coast and eastern Vancouver Island (*www.thesunshinecoast.com*). *Allow 2 to 4 days.*

Begin at Horseshoe Bay, a 30-minute drive northwest from downtown Vancouver, where BC Ferries (tel: 1 888 223 3779; www.bcferries.com) sail the 16km across Howe Sound to Langdale eight times a day.

1 Gibsons

From Langdale, a 3-km (2-mile) long road winds west through forests and farmland along a craggy coastline to Gibsons, the gateway to the Sunshine

Coast. Visitors like to tour Molly's Reach, the set where the television series, *The Beachcombers*, the longest-running show in Canada, was filmed. Other options include a half-hour stroll along the sea walk to a stone cairn marking the spot where Captain Vancouver landed two centuries ago, and studying the Salish native displays and the 25,000 seashells at the Elphinstone Pioneer Museum. West of

Gibsons, just off the main road, are good beaches and hiking trails. Nearby Roberts Creek, a community of artists and artisans, has a camping site right on the water's edge.

2 Sechelt
About 14km northwest of Gibsons stands Sechelt, the commercial centre of the Sunshine Coast. Abundant and colourful marine life entertains scuba divers. Delicacies of the deep are served at the Wharf Restaurants on Davis Bay and at the Blue Heron. The museum at the House of Héwhiwus ('house of chiefs') allows visitors to look back in time. The Sechelt natives, Canada's first self-governing aboriginal group, are renowned for fine carvings and woven cedar baskets.

3 Skookumchuk Narrows
Beyond Sechelt, an hour's hike from Egmont leads to lookouts above the Skookumchuk Narrows, where strong tides (highest during the summer and winter solstices) from three inlets rush at speeds of up to 15 knots through the spectacular rock-strewn passage. A ferry connects nearby Earl's Cove with Saltery Bay across Jervis Inlet, where bald eagles fly overhead and playful killer whales, seals and sea lions compete for slow salmon. Divers can see the bronze mermaid anchored 20m (66 feet) down in Mermaid Cove.

4 Powell River
The next town, Powell River, offers the best salt and freshwater fishing in Canada. The town has the large paper mill which produced Western Canada's first roll of newsprint in 1912.

5 Comox
Four ferries sail daily from Powell River to Comox (dock at Little River) on Vancouver Island, a 75-minute cruise west. Once known for coal mining, now fishing, forestry, farming and tourism sustain the Comox Valley. Visitors come for the sandy beaches, the local handicrafts and the biennial air show. The historic Filbert Lodge and Park is a good place to enjoy afternoon tea followed by a stroll in the gardens.

6 Courtenay
Another interesting place to walk is the adjacent town of Courtenay, where the downtown area has been remodelled with old-fashioned cobblestones and lamps, and brick planters brimming with flowers. The Courtenay Museum and Archives boasts the largest log cabin in the world, built in 1928, where displays of fossils, dolls and Indian artefacts recall times past.

Allow about two hours for the winding road following the coast south to Nanaimo, and the ferry which takes two hours to sail back to Horseshoe Bay.

Waterside restaurant in the Sunshine Circle

Getting away from it all

Stretching in a great quadrangle between the 49th and 60th parallels, Canada's westernmost province brims with options for relaxation, recreation and adventure. Four times the size of Great Britain, BC's great outdoors covers 952,000sq km (367,569sq miles) of mountains and valleys, rivers and lakes, rainforests and deserts, coastlines and islands. Birdwatchers, kayakers and lovers of native Indian art and history like the Queen Charlottes for spotting such species as the rhinoceros auklet, paddling along calm inlets and studying moss-covered totems in abandoned villages.

Fish for something out of the ordinary

The Pacific Ocean washes the shores of BC's main islands, Vancouver Island and the Haida Gwaii (Queen Charlottes). On Vancouver Island, Pacific Rim National Park lures whale watchers and other naturalists to wild beaches. Inland hikers explore the meadows of Forbidden Plateau and Strathcona Provincial Park and the first-growth rainforest in the Carmanah Valley. East of Vancouver, the terrain opens into the Okanagan Valley, where waterslides and wineries flank dude ranches and bird sanctuaries. The valley also has an abundance of apple, cherry and peach orchards. Further east, beyond the good hiking terrain of the Kootenays, stand the majestic Rocky Mountains, a mere 100 million years old, flanking the much older Purcell Mountains. The two became neighbours during the dinosaur era. The Burgess Shale site in **Yoho National Park** contains fossils from an ancient sea. More varieties of life are preserved here, in fantastic detail, than exist in all our modern oceans.

The high interior plateau of the Cariboo Chilcotin attracts equestrians, some of whom head out from the Sundance Guest Ranch on horseback to explore scenic trails, mountain meadows and river valleys. Canadian River Expeditions (*www.canriver.com*) offer a great 11-day circuit, which includes a boat cruise up the coast to Bute Inlet; a float-plane flight over the Homatho Icefield to turquoise Chilko Lake, and a day of fishing and hiking; an exciting raft trip along the Chilko, Chilcotin and Fraser rivers to the town of **Lillooet**; and a scenic return to Vancouver.

North of the Cariboo Chilcotin stretches big-game country. Stewart, Canada's most northerly ice-free port, has recorded up to 27m (89 feet) of snowfall in one year. Winter lures visitors to explore the region by dog sled and Skidoo and on nordic skis, while summer offers boating on **Atlin Lake**, rafting through icebergs on the great Tatshenshini River, and game spotting in Spatsizi Plateau Wilderness Provincial Park.

BC's beaches

BC's 12,000-km (7,456-mile) coastline, dotted with 6,500 islands, boasts lots of beaches, most suitable for sunning, swimming and beachcombing in summer. Vancouver Island is surrounded by beaches, and the Sunshine Coast sports its share, too.

One of the province's most treasured beaches, like many precious things, is fairly remote. Travel to the end of Highway 101 to Lund, north of Powell River on the Sunshine Coast, and take the 15-minute Lund water-taxi ride (*tel: (604) 483 9749*) to Savary Island (*www.savary.online.com*). This crescent-shaped gem is ringed with long beaches, reminiscent of the South Pacific. A warm current mingles with the tides to produce summer waters reaching 22°C (72°F). When Captain Vancouver landed here in 1792, after a long voyage through the South Seas, he admired this island for 'beauty such as we have seldom enjoyed'. The pace of life has not changed much since. The three dozen permanent residents share Savary with

many visitors, especially in summer. They come for the beautiful beaches, the warm waters and the many plants that normally grow much further south.

Near the government wharf, along 'Dough Row', windsurfers skim along with the breeze. Further away from human habitation, beachcombers find a variety of seashells, multicoloured rocks, and perfectly preserved sand dollars. Following the beaches around the island for about 30km (19 miles) is a full day's walk. The perfect way to end the day is with a bite to eat at the Mad Hatter Tea House, a five-minute walk from the government wharf. A sign nearby marks the trail to North America's largest arbutus tree. It takes four adults, arms stretched and touching at the fingertips, to circle the girth.

Visitors who want to linger longer will find two bed-and-breakfast places, but no campsite. Overnighters who insist on sleeping on the beach are warned to watch for changing tides.

Quiet isolated locations are not hard to find

Boating

More than 250,000 BC households have boats. With so many waterways, boating seems as natural as driving. The choices are many and varied, ranging from a simple sunset dinner cruise around English Bay or a passive ride aboard a big BC ferry, to running the rapids of the mighty Fraser River or fishing offshore with whales, sea lions and cormorants for company.

In BC, boating is almost as popular as driving

Desolation Sound

Lund, on the Sunshine Coast (*see p127* for how to get there), and Campbell River, on eastern Vancouver Island, are good starting points for Desolation Sound, 32km (20 miles) north of Powell River. The largest of BC's 32 marine parks, Desolation Sound offers protected warm waters backed by coastal mountains. Native pictographs and coastal lakes make trips ashore interesting, and the waters provide fresh oysters and salmon for dinner.

Okanagan Lake

Okanagan Lake is located in the Okanagan Valley of BC. The lake is neat and clear, 150km (93 miles) long and 300m (984 feet) deep. It is surrounded by mountains and several communities, the largest being Kelowna.

Okanagan Lake has become a popular venue for waterskiing, boating, houseboating and sunbathing at the many surrounding beaches.

It is also home to the Ogopogo, a legend in the Okanagan, which attracts many people from around the world who attempt to capture this 'friendly serpent' on film.

Princess Louisa Inlet

Jervis Inlet, further south on the Sunshine Coast, leads to Princess Louisa Inlet, one of the most scenic fiords in the world. Bordered by craggy granite cliffs streaked with waterfalls and capped with evergreens, the fiord is home to many sea mammals and birds. Erle Stanley Gardner said it best: 'There is no use in describing that inlet. Perhaps an atheist could view it and remain an atheist, but I doubt it.' On top of the gorge is a marine park, crowned by the 40-m (131-foot) high Chatterbox Falls.

The Gulf Islands

Sailing the sheltered waters of the Gulf Islands is also great fun. But watch for 'deadheads', mostly submerged waterlogged tree trunks which have escaped from log booms and could grind your vessel to an untimely halt. Some boat rental companies offer weekend flotilla charters, in which a group of boats sails in the company of a mother ship skippered by a certified instructor. The instructor does the navigating, thus enabling out-of-towners to explore unknown waters with ease. Courses are also offered in basic coastal cruising, coastal navigation, advanced sailing, celestial navigation and offshore sailing.

The Bowron Lakes Circuit

The quietest and most relaxing boating adventure may be the Bowron Lakes circuit, named one of the top 10 canoe trips in the world by *Outside Magazine*. Deep in the heart of the Cariboo Mountains west of the Rockies, this rectangular chain of lakes and connecting waterways is set within a 121,600-hectare (300,480-acre) wilderness park. Along the 116-km (72-mile) route, the placid blue waters reflect glacier-streaked mountains rising to 2,100m (6,890 feet). The region is home to many birds and such other wildlife as moose, bear, lynx and beaver. Paddlers set off from Bowron Lake Lodge and Becker's Lodge, where a variety of canoes and camping gear can be rented. The circuit can be canoed any time from June to October, although June seems to be the best month for seeing both birds and other wildlife.

Shuswap Lake

For a totally different boating holiday, head for the interior town of **Sicamous**, on the Trans-Canada Highway west of Revelstoke. Here, visitors can rent a houseboat, complete with a hot tub on the deck, take the wheel, and head out to tie up at one of 14 beaches on Shuswap Lake. The houseboats are simple to manoeuvre and great fun for families. Houseboaters can swim, fish, and explore the area beneath the Shuswap Highlands from their floating home. *See www.shuswap.bc.ca for information and for places to rent houseboats.*

The Atlin Lake Wilderness

For a boating adventure in the true north, head for Atlin, which lies near the BC/Yukon border. Atlin Lake, which is 100km long, is the place to be in mid-summer when the sun rises at 4.30am and sets at 11.15pm, leaving enough light to take midnight photos. Houseboaters, paddlers and sailors can also go ashore to hike, look for mountain goats, bathe in hot springs and admire alpine scenery.

The best way to get there is to fly to Whitehorse in the Yukon, and rent a car or catch the Atlin Express bus for the three-hour ride south.

If you go

Request the BC Outdoor & Adventure Guide and Charter Boat Adventure brochures from Tourism BC or any BC Travel InfoCentre. Pathways Tours (*tel: (604) 514 8024, toll free (800) 924 2944; www.bowronlakes.com*) organises canoeing tours through the Bowron Lakes for novice paddlers.

Call Yukon Tourism in Whitehorse (*tel: (800) 789 8566; www.touryukon.com*) for information on trips to and on Atlin Lake.

Zodiacs are popular for water tours

Running the rapids

Suddenly a menacing sound rumbles ahead. There is no turning back now. 'Hang on tight!' shouts the boatman. The big rubber raft careens through the foaming rapids. White water slams the pontoons, then gracefully sprays up and falls, and the raft plunges with the flow downstream to calmer waters.

SIMON FRASER

This is rapid-running, but on such chauffeured expeditions, skilled rapid-runners man the oars. The rafts are not easy to capsize, but passengers wear life jackets, just in case. In rough water, the raft may buck and leap like a Wild West bronco. River-running is not always a dry experience, so it is best to keep cameras in waterproof bags.

River-running is more than just navigating rivers. Most trips allow time for hikes ashore and a cooling swim in the river. On longer trips, the boatmen may become chefs and grill salmon steaks or hamburgers over an open fire, while the aroma of freshly brewed coffee fills the air. Often a happy evening can be spent around a campfire chatting with new-found friends, with time left over to gaze at the moon and stars

before settling in for the night.

The mighty Fraser River
Several powerful rivers surge through BC, carrying such Indian names as Chilko and Chehalis (meaning 'where the chest of a canoe grounds on a sandbar'), and honouring such early explorers as Thompson and Fraser. But the Fraser River is the greatest of them all.

Rising as a trickle in the southeast corner of Mount Robson Provincial Park in the Rockies, the Fraser travels 1,280km southwest to empty into the Pacific. From Mount Robson, the river flows fast and pristine to Quesnel, where the blue waters turn turgid brown, due, at least in part, to chemical waste of pulp mills. There are rapids at Scuzzy Rock, China Bar and **Hell's Gate** – appropriately named, for here the mighty

Simon Fraser was an American-born fur trader and explorer for the North West Company. He was also one of the great river-runners of the 19th century.

In 1808, against the advice of the native Indians, he led an expedition in birch-bark canoes down a river he believed to be the Columbia. He was mistaken, and that fast river of many rapids and deep gorges now bears his name.

At Hell's Gate, Fraser wrote: 'It is so wild that I cannot find words to describe our situation at times . . . a desperate undertaking!'

His persistent and perilous journey changed the map of the continent.

Fraser churns through a narrow, glacially carved 34-m (112-foot) wide gorge. As the raft runs from Boston Bar for 42km (26 miles) down to Yale, the boatman usually gives a running commentary on the mining history of the area.

For a more gentle trip, boaters start at Hope and wend their way past New Westminster to the Oak Street Bridge in Vancouver. This shows how the city is developing close to the river.

The Creston Valley

Another gentle journey is the one- to three-day canoe trip through the Creston Valley (*www.crestonvalley.com*). Paddlers start at the Canada/US border on Highway 21 and go north with the flow to Kootenay Lake. Protected marshlands make for safe canoeing.

More than 250 species of birds inhabit or visit the valley, and the area between Creston and Nelson is home to 140 pairs of osprey, one of the largest osprey nesting sites in the world.

Contact the Creston Valley Wildlife Management Centre (*tel: (250) 402*

6900; www.crestonwildlife.ca) for more canoeing information.

The Chilko River

Another exciting rafting trip follows Chilko River which falls into three sections. The run is a gentle one from Chilko Lake to Lava Canyon, where sets of grade-five rapids await the rafter. The last stretch runs from the Taseko River junction to the Chilcotin River junction. *www.chilcotin.bc.ca*

Chilliwack River Rafting Adventures
Tel: toll free 1 800 410 7238; www.dowco.com/chilliwackrafting
Fraser River Raft Expeditions Ltd
Tel: (800) 363 RAFT; www.fraserraft.com
Hyak Wilderness Adventures
Tel: (604) 734 8622, toll free (800) 663 RAFT; www.hyak.com
Kumsheen Raft Adventures
Tel: (250) 455 2296, toll free (800) 663 6667; www.kumsheen.com
Whistler River Adventures
Tel: (604) 932 3532, toll free (888) 932 3532; www.whistlerriver.com

Rafters need skill and courage to brave the rapids

Riding the rails

A few years ago, the *Pacific Coast Starlight*, the *Cariboo Prospector* and the *Whistler Northwind* were gone in one fell swoop when BC Rail ceased to exist. But rail travel is so much a part of BC's history and soul that new journeys were bound to loom on the horizon before long. And so they have: in 2006, the *Whistler Mountaineer* is launched, a spanking new 3-hour rail trip along the 'Sea-to-Sky' route that follows the coastline from Vancouver to Whistler. Like its very successful parent, the *Rocky Mountaineer* that runs from Vancouver to Banff and Jasper, the *Whistler Mountaineer* will offer the finest in local cuisine served against the panoramic mountain and coastal scenery.

Thundering through snowcapped mountains

Operated by Rocky Mountaineer Vacations, the 'old timer' *Rocky Mountaineer* ride through British Columbia to the Rockies has been dubbed one of the most spectacular rail tours in the world. Passengers come again and again – says one Brit, 'You think you've seen it all and then you come around a bend and it's even better than what you saw before.' Although travel could be done in a day, the *Rocky Mountaineer* takes two days so that passengers can soak in the maximum eye-popping views during daylight hours. On the first day, the biggest 'wows' come through the Fraser Canyon; on the second day, it's the Rockies. On-board entertainment is part of the ride, but the best bit is the running commentary by staff members who pride themselves on knowing absolutely everything and delivering their facts with humour and drama.

During the journey, lush rainforests are punctuated by deep canyons and raging waterfalls. There are lakes and forests, painted deserts, dramatic bridges high above rivers, tunnels, glaciers and soaring mountain peaks. Most people opt to do the trip during the spring, summer and autumn months but there's also a winter ride into the Rockies through the Land of a Million Christmas Trees. It's rumoured Santa even comes on board.

Vancouver is also the Western terminus for VIA Rail's *Canadian*, a continuous trip from the coast to Toronto, taking in the full panorama of Canada's distinct geographic changes. Seeing the country with VIA is a once-in-a-lifetime dream for many visitors. VIA's *Skeena* also follows a northerly route across the middle of the province from Prince Rupert to Jasper.

Riding the trails

Horse riding is an easy and pleasant way to explore BC outdoors. Riding appeals to almost all ages: the views can be marvellous, the pace therapeutic and the environmental impact minimal. Because the animals carry the gear, horseback holidays have extra appeal for families with young children who might find arduous hikes overwhelming. Most BC outfitters and dude ranchers use placid quarter horses and Arabian stock for trekking. They have comfortable gaits and respond to neck reining, which allows one hand free to hang on to the saddle horn.

In the Lower Mainland, latent cowpokes can canter in Golden Ears Park. Professional stables guide riders out of Maple Ridge (*www.mapleridge.com*) for a day trek to Alouette Lake, where they can hitch their horses to a tree and go for a swim. Several hundred kilometres of trails in **Manning Park** (*www.manningparkresort.com*) are ideal for ambling through Canada's mountainous west. Late summer or autumn is a good season to ride, as the insects retreat and the autumn leaves turn bright red, rust and yellow. In mid-September at Manning, the alpine larch trees on Frosty Mountain turn a deep gold before dropping their deciduous needles.

North of Vancouver, at **Williams Lake** (*www.chilcotin.bc.ca*), riders can head west to **Tatlayoko Lake** in the Chilcotin for week-long journeys to see ice caves, fossil beds and meadows where grizzly bears forage in the Potato Mountain Coast Range. East of Williams Lake,

riders can overnight at Helmcken Falls Lodge (*tel: (250) 674 3657; www.helmckenfall.com*) near Clearwater and ride lodge horses along the trails of Wells Gray Park.

For unusual trekking, try remote **Mount Edziza Park** (contact the Skeena District in Smithers, *tel: (250) 847 7320*), where the Tahltan Indians introduce riders to moonscapes of cinder cones and mountains of shale, occasionally pockmarked by hungry grizzlies hunting gophers. Any saddle sores suffered during the long trek may be soothed by hellebore root, which the guide boils up in an old tin can.

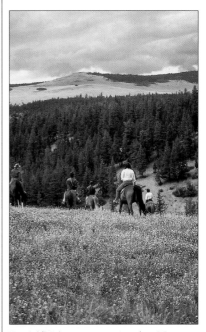

Horse riding is a great way to explore BC

The history of the railway in Canada is the history of the development of this sprawling, rugged land. The CPR was founded in 1881 and it took 54 months to complete. The last spike was driven in Craigellahire, BC, in 1885. The line connects Montreal with Port Moody, BC, a distance of 4,627km (2,875 miles).

Where the iron horse ambled, settlers and prosperity usually followed. The first scheduled passenger train arrived in Vancouver in 1887. The arrival of the railway energised the economy of the Pacific Northwest, bringing large numbers of Canadians and Europeans. The population of Vancouver mushroomed from 900 to 8,000 within five years, and the Canadian Pacific Railway (*www.cprheritage.com*) became the city's largest employer.

The CPR built the first Hotel Vancouver, bought and sold land, operated sternwheelers on BC rivers and ran steamships across the Pacific Ocean.

Freight trains running across the country encouraged the exploitation of natural resources. Such BC products as fur, coal, lumber, gold and fish suddenly found accessible markets.

The transcontinental train service has been curtailed in recent years, since cars and trucks, along with aircraft and helicopters, have diminished passenger demand. Most British Columbians now drive or fly to get from one place to another, but holidaymakers still love the romance and the rattle of the rails, the gentle pace, and the friendliness of the conductors and other passengers from all over the world.

Yet the scenery remains the greatest attraction. Early CPR President Cornelius Van Horne commented back in 1895, 'Since we cannot export the scenery, we shall have to import the tourists'. Rail travellers love the stillness and splendour of the unfolding wilderness panorama of mountains, canyons, lakes, rivers, streams, forests and rolling ranchlands, and glimpses of such elusive wildlife as deer, elk, moose, bighorn sheep and bear. They love the dramatic spiral tunnel near Kicking Horse Pass; the geography lesson, and whistle stops at remote towns and villages; and the sense of pioneer adventure.

Some useful websites giving information on scenic tours across Canada are: *www.cprtours.com*, *www.viarail.ca* and *www.rkymtnrail.com*

Railway personnel keep the tracks in good condition for the trains' safe passage, and look after their passengers, too

Provincial parks

There are more than 450 provincial parks in BC, encompassing glaciers, grasslands, rainforests, rivers, lakes, dormant volcanoes, mountains, islands, fiords and beaches. There are over 2,000km (1,243 miles) of hiking trails, and more than 90 parks with good canoeing and hiking, some with good fishing and some with boat launches. More than 12,000 pitches in 175 campgrounds are scattered throughout the parks. Several have interpretative programmes, so visitors can hear talks about flora and fauna and star-gaze with astronomers. Parks cover more than 5 per cent of BC, an area larger than the province of Nova Scotia. For more information visit *www.elp.gov.bc.ca/bcparks* or call BC Parks in Valemort at *(250) 566 4325*.

Superb mountain scenery surrounds trekkers wherever they go

Mount Robson Provincial Park

A favourite with many adventurers, Mount Robson Provincial Park contains the highest peak (3,954m/12,972 feet) in the Canadian Rockies, the headwaters of the Fraser River and spectacular scenery, but has limited access. From June to September, visitors admire more than 50 species of alpine flowers, 170 species of birds (including golden eagles), grizzly bears, caribou, mountain goats and hoary marmots. Robson Helimagic (*tel: (250) 566 4700, toll free (877) 454 4700; www.robsonhelimagic.com*) runs heli-hikes into the park for people of all ages. The base camp, at 2,073m (6,801 feet), nestles in a rain shadow surrounded by flowering meadows and snowy peaks.

Pure water flows in glacier-fed streams. Hikers bathe downstream in natural pools and waterfalls, and spend about six hours each day exploring the wilderness. After an evening slide show in the main mess tent, the Northern Lights sometimes brighten the darkening sky. (*www.mountrobsonlodge.com*)

Strathcona Park

BC's oldest park boasts six of the seven highest peaks on Vancouver Island, along with the Comox Glacier, the island's last remaining icefield, thus earning the nickname 'Little Switzerland'. Although Strathcona is truly a wilderness park, day trippers take the half-hour drive west from Courtenay in the Comox Valley in summer to enjoy the alpine flowers and hike the Forbidden Plateau.

Available accommodation includes campgrounds at Buttle Lake and Ralph River, and the Strathcona Lodge (*tel: (250) 286 3122; www.strathcona.bc.ca*), on the lake just outside the park. The lodge's superb outdoor education centre offers apprenticeships in wilderness leadership, rock climbing, mountaineering, white-water canoeing, kayaking and photographing wildlife. Experienced hikers enjoy the Flower Ridge, Elk River and Marble Meadows trails radiating out from Buttle Lake, as well as the challenge of scaling the 2,200-m (7,218-foot) Golden Hinde. Della Falls, the continent's highest at 440m (1,444 feet), are located in the southern part of the park. Visitors take a water-taxi from the Ark Resort (*tel: (250) 723 2657; www.arkresort.com*) near Port Alberni up Great Central Lake and then hike 16km (10 miles) to the falls. (*www.strathconapark.com*)

Tweedsmuir Provincial Park
This is BC's largest park. Many overseas visitors rent campers in Vancouver, drive north to Williams Lake on the Cariboo Highway (97), and then west on the Freedom Highway (20) to Bella Coola. This route runs through southern Tweedsmuir Park. Hair-raising switchbacks lead down into the **Atnarko River Valley**, a good location for day hikes into the Rainbow Mountains.

The Rainbow Mountain Outfitting (*tel: (250) 742 3539; www.rainbowadventuresbc.com*) of Anahim Lake, guides in these parts for three generations, come highly recommended for week-long horseback outings during July and August. The Hunlen Lakes area, which provides excellent canoeing, is where the pioneer settler Ralph Edwards helped save trumpeter swans from extinction during the 1950s. Ralph's son John runs the Hunlen Wilderness Camp.

Wells Gray Provincial Park
Considered one of BC's finest parks, it is located just north of Clearwater, a five-hour drive north from Vancouver on Highway 5. The park offers great hiking in summer and hut-to-hut skiing in winter. Clearwater Lake is easily accessible and offers good beaches and good fishing. In winter, the 142-m (466-foot) Helmcken Falls freeze into a 20-storey ice cone, broader at the base than a football field. Helmcken Falls Lodge (*tel: (250) 674 3657; www.helmckenfalls.com*) was originally built as a hunting lodge at the entrance to the park. Visitors love it as a base for hiking, canoeing, backpacking, horse riding, mountaineering, glacier exploration and fishing.
Thompson River District.
Tel: (250) 851 3000.

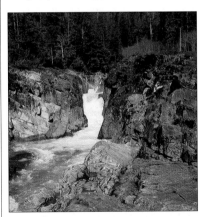

Waterfalls appear beside the road, here between Ucluelet and Tofino

The Rockies

This mountainous region of outstanding scenic splendour stretches northwest for 1,400km (870 miles) along the BC-Alberta border. It is bounded on the east by vast prairies and on the west by the Rocky Mountain Trench, one of the longest valleys in the world. Most of the Rocky Mountains are in Alberta. For much of their length, they form the Continental Divide separating Canada's east- and west-flowing rivers.

Mountain terrain near Banff

Mount Robson, the highest peak, shoots 4,000m (13,123 feet) skyward, while Mount Assiniboine, the Matterhorn of Canada, is a breathtaking 3,600-m (11,811-foot) tusk of layered rock carved into a pyramid shape by glacial cirques.

The Rockies were created about 65 million years ago, when the land uplifted and broke along great fault lines, forcing the rock to fold and buckle. During the last Ice Age, about 12,000 years ago, glaciers completed this sculpting by nature.

The Kootenay Indians have lived here for 10,000 years. As hunters and gatherers, they knew all the secret passes through the mountains. When the explorer and fur trader David Thompson eventually struggled through Howes Pass in 1807, the Kootenays nicknamed him 'Star Man'.

Although other explorers and traders, prospectors, missionaries and homesteaders (pioneer farmers) followed, few settled. The discovery of gold at Wild Horse Creek in 1863 brought a surge of 5,000 souls, but when the gold was gone only about 20 families remained. Two decades later, the Northwest Mounted Police established a detachment here, headed by Superintendent Samuel Steele.

Today, the area is a haven for the adventure tourist, who heads here in passionate pursuit of the peaks and the outdoor action. The air is fresh, the waters clear and the scenery awesome. From such guest ranches as Top of the World, Beaverfoot and Bull River, visitors can canter around the countryside all day and return to find freshly caught rainbow trout sizzling on the grill. Others may prefer to hike over alpine meadows, play golf or paddle, sail, windsurf or waterski on emerald lakes. Or they may savour the silvery cascades of Laughing Falls, or soak in warmer water at the Radium, Fairmont or Lussin hot springs.

Wildlife watchers, especially at dawn and dusk, may spot moose, deer, elk, mountain goat, bear, lynx, coyote and marmots. Winter resorts offer nordic and alpine skiing, while heli-skiing (helicopter skiing) in the Bugaboo area is an experience of a lifetime.

Fort Steele

At this fine historic heritage town, the gold-mining past is vividly present in over 60 reconstructed buildings. Highlights include ice-cream making, stagecoach rides, recreated old newspapers, Victorian vaudeville at the Wildhorse Theatre and workers costumed as blacksmiths, carpenters, quilters and weavers.

The town is 16km (10 miles) northeast of Cranbrook. Tel: (250) 426 7352, 24-hour hotline. Open: daily sunrise–sunset. Admission charge.

Kimberley

Canada's highest city at 1,117m (3,665 feet) Kimberley is nicknamed the 'Bavarian City of the Rockies'. The red-brick pedestrian Platzl holds the world's largest operating cuckoo clock. Bavarian-style buildings sport dark wood panelling, floral decorations and window boxes filled with red geraniums. European delis and restaurants serve such German specialities as *Weisswurst*, *Spetzle* and *Strudel*. Kimberley has been a zinc-, silver- and lead-mining town since the 1890s. A 20-minute train ride carries visitors in an old mining car through a tunnel and over a trestle.

For information on accommodation, tel: (250) 427 3922, toll free (800) 667 0871; www.kimberleyvacations.bc.ca

Kootenay National Park

Here, a half-hour hike through moss-carpeted forest leads to the Paint Pots, ponds stained red, orange and yellow by iron oxide which the Kootenay Indians used for body and rock painting.

Located south of Yoho National Park. Open year-round. Tel: (250) 343 6783.

Yoho National Park

With 28 peaks more than 3,000m (9,843 feet) high, all layered with rock, blue ice and snow, this park offers such varied sights as the Takakkaw Falls, the spiral railway tunnels leading up to Kicking Horse Pass and the Burgess Shale fossil beds, which include petrified remains of 120 species, dating as far back as 530 million years.

Located just west of the Continental Divide and Banff National Park. Open year-round.

Banff and Jasper National Park (Alberta)

Canada's oldest national park, Banff was established in 1885 after hot springs were seen gushing from the side of Sulphur Mountain. The main resort towns are Banff, named after Banffshire in Scotland, and Lake Louise, located at the Continental Divide.

Jasper National Park, the largest designated parkland in the Rocky Mountains, lies north of Banff and west of Edmonton. Scenic highlights include Mount Edith Cavell and Maligne Lake, a large and beautiful remnant of a retreating glacier. The Columbia Icefield, a glacier that has not yet retreated, is about an hour's drive south. *(See www.banffnationalpark.com)*

For further information, contact: the Rocky Mountain Visitors Association at *PO Box 10, Kimberley, BC V1A 2Y5. Tel: (250) 427 4838*; or Tourism Rockies at *tel: (250) 427 4838; www.kootenayrockies.com*

Pick up some of BC's ice wines as a souvenir

Shopping

Western Canadians have been shopping in Vancouver ever since the Oppenheimer brothers began outfitting prospectors and homesteaders more than a century ago. The range of goods has, of course, expanded far beyond the dreams of those early settlers, and sturdy outdoor clothing is as much a fashion item as a necessity these days.

The high standard of living and high expectations of its citizens have made Vancouver a wonderful place to shop – and prices are often lower than in Europe. There are shops everywhere, from the heritage areas of Gastown to the modern, underground Pacific Centre mall; from the colourful markets to the trendy designer boutiques.

In addition to all the usual shopping mall and high-street retailers, there are specialist stores for just about everything: items for left-handed people, clothes for short or tall people, shoes for big feet, pewter ware, cigars, artistic chocolates, etc.

The eclectic range of goods is also broadened by the diverse cultures of the immigrant populations.

Robson Street is the hub of it all – the most popular strolling street in Vancouver – where people meet and greet, gaze at store windows filled with clothes and curios from around the globe, and linger in the cafés and restaurants to watch the world go by. On Friday evenings in summer, there is open-air ballroom dancing to live music in Robson Square (*tel: (604) 925 5003*). The other main shopping streets are Water Street in Gastown, Pender Street in Chinatown and South Granville Street for art, antiques and carpets.

Arts and crafts

Canoe Pass Gallery
The work of gifted Canadian Native artists is on display in this heritage-village gallery, including masks, carvings, prints, jewellery and sculpture.
3866 Bayview St, Steveston.
Tel: (604) 272 0095.

Coastal Peoples Fine Arts Gallery
Native artwork, including gold and silver jewellery, masks, totem poles, paintings, prints and Inuit sculptures.
1072 Mainland St, Yaletown.
Tel: (604) 685 9298.

Crafthouse
The gallery of the Crafts Association of British Columbia, with items chosen to represent a spirit of exploration and a tradition of quality.
1386 Cartwright St, Granville Island.
Tel: (604) 687 7270.

Hill's Native Art
An enormous selection of native art and craft work.
165 Water St, Gastown. Tel: (604) 685 4249. Also at 1008 Government St, Victoria (tel: (604) 385 3911); and at 76 Bastion St, Nanaimo (tel: (604) 755 7873).

Jade World

Visitors can watch the craft workers here turning rough boulders into beautiful, translucent jade sculptures, carvings and jewellery for sale.
1696 W 1st Ave. Tel: (604) 733 7212.

Khot-la-cha

Authentic Coast Salish handicrafts on sale include carvings, moose-hide crafts, clothing and porcupine-quill jewellery.
270 Whonoak St, North Vancouver.
Tel: (604) 987 3339.

Trading Post

Native artists still come to this restored 1911 log cabin near the famous Capilano suspension bridge to sell their work. Items include spirit masks, jewellery, knitwear and leatherware.
3735 Capilano Rd, North Vancouver.
Tel: (604) 985 7474. Open: daily.

Clothing

Angel

The clothing here is described as 'wearable art', with hand-painted garments for children and adults.
2 Powell St. Tel: (604) 681 0947.

Diana Sanderson Studio

Fine quality, hand-dyed and woven silk clothing, accessories and jewellery.
1551 Johnston St, Granville Island.
Tel: (604) 687 7455.

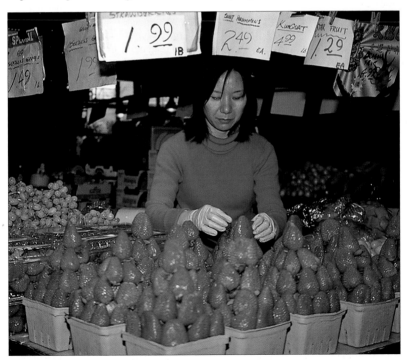

The fragrance of fresh fruit can be intoxicating at Granville Island's public market

Leather Ranch

A huge selection of quality leather and
suede fashions and accessories.
856 Granville St. Tel: (604) 669 9188.
Also at Guildford Town Centre, Surrey
(tel: (604) 584 7044); and Eaton Centre
in Victoria (tel: (250) 384 4217).

OK Boot Corral

Western boots, hats, belts, buckles, bolo
ties and souvenirs of the old west.
205 Carrall St, Gastown.
Tel: (604) 684 BOOT (2668).

Repp Big and Tall

Casual and smart clothing for big, tall
guys, with tailoring available on the
premises for quick alterations.
475 West Hastings St. Tel: (604) 681
3548. Open: Mon–Sat 9am–5.30pm;
Sun noon–5pm.

Roots Canada

Established in 1973, Roots now has
more than 80 stores across the country,
selling its own line of rugged, casual
clothing for the family, including leather
jackets, outerwear, footwear and athletic
wear.
Pacific Centre, 701 West Georgia St.
Tel: (604) 408 4250. Also at 1001 Robson
at Burrard St (tel: (604) 683 4305); and
Metrotown Centre, Burnaby (tel: (604
435 5554).

Tall Girl

This store offers fashion, sportswear,
footwear, lingerie and sleepwear, in a
range of sizes all designed for tall, long-
waisted or long-legged figures.
644 Hornby St. Tel: (604) 688 9238.
Also at 709 Yates St, Victoria (tel: (250)
388 7034).

Tilley Endurables

Travel and adventure clothing, including
the famous Tilley hat – it floats, ties on,

Shopping for those with a sweet tooth on
fashionable Robson Street

repels rain, won't shrink and comes with
a lifetime guarantee and a four-page
owner's manual!
2401 Granville St & 8th St.
Tel: (604) 732 4287. Open: Mon–Sat
10am–5.30pm, Sun noon–5pm.

True Value Vintage Clothing

You can buy, sell, trade and rent vintage
clothing here, or you can just browse
around the range of garments and
accessories from the 1920s to the '70s.
710 Robson St. Tel: (604) 685 5403.

Duty-free shopping

Tourists are eligible for a rebate on
certain goods that will be taken outside
the country within 60 days of purchase.
The easiest way to benefit from the
scheme is to shop at a duty-free outlet,
where instant reductions of up to 60 per
cent are available on the price of
qualifying items, including liquor,
cigarettes, perfume, cosmetics and
designer merchandise. Otherwise, you
have to wait until you get home before
applying for the rebate. Information is
available at duty-free outlets.

Spirit of the North Duty Free
*1026 Alberni St, Vancouver. Tel: (604)
683 2416.*

Gifts, souvenirs and specialist stores
Accent on Pewter
A vast selection of pewtercraft,
including jewellery and tableware.
*1289 Robson St. Tel: (604) 683 5799.
Open: daily 10am–6pm (9pm Thur &
10pm Fri), Sun noon–6pm.*
Chocolate Arts
Chocolate medallions with Haida
designs.

*2037 West 4th Ave. Tel: (604) 739 0475.
Open: Mon–Sat 10am–6pm, Sun
noon–5pm.*
Crash
Contemporary home furnishings for the
spacially challenged.
*1551 Johnston St. Tel: (604) 684 9922.
Open: daily 9.30am–6pm.*
Lululemon Athletica
Trendy yoga apparel with a designer
West Coast twist.
*1148 Robson St. Tel: (604) 681 3118;
www.lululemon.com*

Shoppers can browse well into the evening

Dagoli
Local artist Dagoli's outlet for his own
line of 'Ancient Cave Art' T-shirts. Also
craft jewellery and whimsical gift items.
1915 Stainsbury Ave. Tel: (604) 254 8330.
Open: daily 10am–6pm.

Grand Maple
Quality Canadian souvenirs, including a
large collection of BC jade and, of
course, maple syrup.
1046 Robson St. Tel: (604) 681 8979.

The Umbrella Shop
Now into its third generation, this
family business has an in-house factory
making a large selection of umbrellas to
complement the imported ones.
1160 W Broadway. Tel: (604) 669 9444.
*Open Mon–Fri 9.30am–5.30pm, Sat
10am–5pm.*

Markets
Vancouver's markets are lively and
entertaining places to shop. In a party
atmosphere of street entertainment and
fast food, you can browse around stalls
selling Canadian crafts, souvenirs,
designer kitchenware, flowers and all
kinds of fresh produce.

Granville Island Market
The oldest of several waterfront
markets, this one is on a broad outdoor
deck overlooking the marine activity in
False Creek.
*On Granville Island; accessible by AquaBus
(tel: (604) 689 5858) from the foot of
Granville St. Open: Tue–Sun 9am–6pm.*

Lonsdale Quay Market
Highlights among the wide selection
of goods available are Harriet's House,
for handmade quilts and toys, and
Out of Africa for African crafts and
clothing.

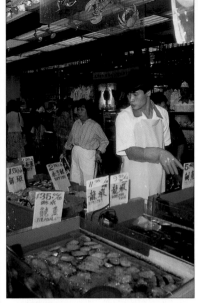
A street stall in Chinatown

*123 Carrie Cates Court, North
Vancouver; accessible by SeaBus from
downtown. Tel: (604) 985 6261.*
*Open: daily 9.30am–6.30pm
(9pm on Fri).*

Park Royal Market
Visiting Park Royal is like doing a tour
of Europe, with its Belgian bakery,
German deli, Italian pasta outlets,
Scottish butcher and international news-
stand.
*Park Royal South, Marine Drive, West
Vancouver. Tel: (604) 922 3211.*
*Open: Mon–Sat 9.30am–5.30pm
(9pm on Thur & Fri), Sun noon–6pm.*

Robson Market
On the upstairs level, artisan-vendors
and a cluster of cafés have the
impressive backdrop of a 43m-long
mural depicting life in the West End –
all overlooking the colourful displays of
produce below.
1610 Robson St. Tel: (604) 682 2733.
Open: daily 9am–9pm.

Vancouver Flea Market
Over 360 stalls vie for business in the city's largest flea market, where you can bargain for unusual souvenirs.
703 Terminal Ave, five-minute walk from Main St. Tel: (604) 685 0666.
Open: Sat–Sun & holidays 9am–5pm.
Westminster Quay Market
Getting here is half the fun, involving a spectacular 30-minute ride by Sky-Train from downtown. The market overlooks the Fraser River.

810 Quayside. Tel: (604) 520 3881.
Open: daily 9.30am–6.30pm.

Shopping malls
The Landing
This beautifully restored heritage building houses an exceptional range of elegant fashion stores and speciality goods, and a selection of fine restaurants.
375 Water St. Tel: (604) 483 5050.

Bonsai trees are only one of dozens of crafted items sold at Salt Spring's market

Landsdowne Park

Five minutes' drive from the airport, this mall has over 120 shops, including department stores, designer fashions and many speciality shops. There is also an indoor children's playground.
No 3 Rd at Alderbridge Way, Richmond. Tel: (604) 270 1344. Open: Mon–Tue & Sat 9am–5.30pm, Wed–Fri 9.30am–9pm, Sun noon–5pm.

Metrotown Centre

Greater Vancouver's largest shopping complex, just 15 minutes from downtown, with over 500 stores. All the big names and plenty of independents are represented here, and there are special events to entertain shoppers. The centre has different attractions: **Playdium** (*tel: (604) 434 6522;*

www.playdium.com) is full of games and virtual reality. **Metropolis** is where Playdium is located. It also has silverscreen cinemas and IMAX. **Eaton Centre**, attached to Metrotown, has many fashion stores. Station Square has the **Holiday Inn** (*tel: (604) 438 1881*) and cinemas (*tel: (604) 433 8438*).
4800 Kingsway, Burnaby. Open: Mon–Fri 10am–9pm, Sat 9.30am–6pm, Sun 11am–5.30pm.

Oakridge Centre

Over 150 quality stores here enjoy a bright and airy environment, with 20-m (66-foot) high vaulted skylights. There is also a cineplex.
41st Ave at Cambie St. Tel: (604) 261 2511. Open Mon–Sat 9.30am–6pm (Wed–Fri 9pm), Sun noon–5pm.

There are plenty of places to shop for souvenirs

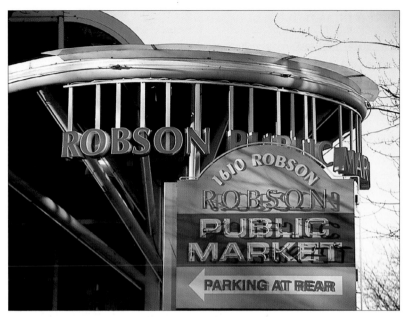

Take in the public market on Robson Street

Pacific Centre Mall
This mall spreads over and under three downtown city blocks, where a three-storey waterfall, a glass rotunda and a skylighted atrium attempt to bring the outdoors indoors. Anchored by the big department stores, Eaton's and The Bay, the mall has about 160 other stores.
At Georgia and Howe sts. Tel: (604) 688 7236. Open: Mon–Sat 9.30am–7pm (Thur & Fri 9pm, Sat 6pm), Sun noon–6pm.

Park Royal Mall
This mall opened more than 40 years ago, when it was Canada's first major shopping centre. It has over 200 stores, half of which are independent traders. Other attractions include cinemas, bowling lanes and a golf driving range.
At the foot of the Lions Gate Bridge in West Vancouver. Tel: (604) 922 3211. Open: Mon–Sat 10am–6pm (Thur & Fri 9pm); Sun noon–6pm.

Richmond Centre
All the usual department stores and international chains are gathered in this large mall near the airport.
No 3 Rd & Westminster Highway. Infoline tel: (604) 713 7467. Open: Mon–Sat 9.30am–6pm (Wed–Fri until 9pm), Sun 11am–6pm.

Sinclair Centre
This restored historic building houses a small cluster of exclusive shops circling an elegant skylit atrium, where musicians entertain and artists display their works.
757 West Hastings St. www.sinclaircentre. com. Open: Mon–Sat 10am–5.30pm.

Entertainment

Few people come to Vancouver for entertainment, except for the outdoor variety so bountifully offered by Mother Nature. But Vancouver is a quietly vibrant city and does offer such various indoor options as ballet, opera, classical music, rock, jazz, theatre and cinema, featuring respectable local, national and international talent.

Dance performance at the Cowichan Native Heritage Centre

The daily newspapers, *The Vancouver Sun* (*www.canada.com/vancouversun*) and *The Province* (*www.canada.com/theprovince*), along with the free weeklies, *The West Ender* and *Georgia Strait*, contain advertising and editorial reviews of current entertainment. *WHERE Vancouver* (*www.wherevancouver.com*), a compact monthly magazine free in most hotels, provides details of musical and theatrical performances, along with listings of cabarets, clubs and jazz gigs.

The **Arts Hotline** (*tel: (604) 681 3535; www.allianceforarts.com*) provides information on the performing arts, and the **Coastal Jazz and Blues Society** (*tel: (604) 872 5200; www.coastaljazz.ca*) offers information on the jazz scene.

For recorded information on current movies and cinema locations, call **Cineplex Odeon** (*tel: (604) 684 4000*), **Famous Players** (*tel: (604) 669 6000*), or the individual independent cinemas.

All kinds of street entertainers are scattered throughout the city, but especially on Robson Street. However, the best shows usually materialise on Granville Island on sunny Sunday afternoons. Here, on the wooden deck in front of the market overlooking False Creek, jugglers, clowns, storytellers, mime artists and musicians vie for attention. More formal outdoor concerts are held on Grouse Mountain and at Dr Sun Yat-Sen Garden on Carrall Street (*tel: (604) 689 7133*).

Tickets

Ticketmaster (*tel: (604) 280 4444; www.ticketmaster.ca*), which has outlets in Eaton's department store at downtown Pacific Centre and at information counters in major malls throughout the city, sells tickets for cultural and sporting events. Ticketmaster has special lines for arts events (*tel: (604) 280 3311*) and spectator sports (*tel: (604) 280 4400*).

Ballet, opera and classical music

Ballet BC (*tel: (604) 732 5003*), **Canada's Royal Winnipeg Ballet** and such well-known visiting dance companies as the Kiev Ballet perform at the 2,800-seat Queen Elizabeth Theatre, at 630 Hamilton Street.

Also at the Queen Elizabeth, the **Vancouver Opera** (*tel: (604) 682 2871*) and visiting opera companies present contemporary productions and such timeless masterpieces as *The Marriage of*

Figaro and *Don Pasquale*. At the adjacent **Vancouver Playhouse** (*tel: (604) 665 3050*), the **Vancouver East Cultural Centre** (*tel: (604) 251 1363*), or, as it's affectionately known to locals, 'the Cultch', has an impressive programme of avant-garde theatre, international music, festivals and other arts events.

Many musical events are also held at the gracious and elegant **Orpheum**, located at 884 Granville, Smythe at Seymour (*tel: (604) 665 3035*). The Orpheum is the home of the **Vancouver Symphony Orchestra** (*Infoline: (604) 876 3434*), which also performs at various other Lower Mainland venues and at several outdoor locations during the summer.

Several classical chamber music groups run by professional musicians present complimentary concerts at a number of public sites. Free lunchtime concerts are often held on the plaza in Robson Square and in shopping malls around the city during July and August.

Headphones for people with hearing impairment are available at the Queen Elizabeth Theatre, the Vancouver Playhouse and the Orpheum. All these places are wheelchair-accessible. *For more information on Vancouver theatres, call (604) 665 3050, or visit www.city.vancouver.bc.ca/theatres*

Vancouver is home to many musical performances, big and small

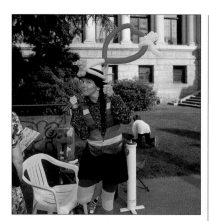

A street performer outside the Vancouver Art Gallery

Jazz

There are many good jazz artists and good places to enjoy them in Vancouver (*www.jazzvancouver.com*). Evenings offer a good choice, including the **Arts Club Backstage Lounge** at 1585 Johnston Street (*tel: (604) 687 1354*). The **Cellar Restaurant Jazz Club**, on 3611 W. Broadway (*tel: (604) 738 1959*), features blues and cool jazz with name players and new talent. **Café Deux Soleils**, 2096 Commercial Drive (*tel: (604) 254 1195*), is the home of live entertainment, the schedule of which is subject to frequent change. The annual **Vancouver International Jazz Festival** is held throughout Vancouver in late June. For more information, call the **Jazz Hotline** (*tel: (604) 872 5200*) or visit *www.jazzvancouver.com*

Rock and contemporary music

Big Canadian and international names entertain regularly at **BC Place Stadium** (*tel: (604) 661 7242*) which seats 60,000 people; **Thunderbird Stadium** at 6081 Thunderbird Boulevard at the UBC campus (*tel: (604) 822 6121*), the **Pacific Coliseum** (*tel: (604) 253 2311*) by the Pacific National Exhibition grounds, and **GM Place** (*tel: (604) 899 7889*) – also known as The Garage, and home to Canuck's NHL Hockey Team for Vancouver.

Smaller places to hear good rock and local talent include the **Railway Club**, at 519 Dunsmuir (*tel: (604) 681 1625*), and **Richards** at 1036 Richards Street (*tel: (604) 687 6794*).

Theatre

The **Arts Club Theatre** (*tel: (604) 687 5315; www.artsclub.com*) offers the best in live theatre, ranging from classical Shakespeare to popular drama and contemporary works created by local playwrights. Programmes are presented year-round at the Mainstage and Revue theatres on Granville Island. Also on Granville Island, the **Waterfront Theatre** (*tel: (604) 685 1731*) stages outstanding Canadian plays, while the adjacent **Carousel Theatre** (*tel: (604) 669 3410*) entertains youngsters. The **Vancouver Playhouse** (*tel: (604) 665 3050*), housed in the same building as the **Queen Elizabeth Theatre** at 630 Hamilton Street downtown, stages six full-scale productions each season, including classic and contemporary drama, comedy, musicals and at least one Canadian play. **Theatre Under The Stars** (*tel: (604) 687 0174; e-mail for information: tutsbc@telus.net*) has been putting on Broadway-style musicals for half a century at the Malkin Bowl bandstand outdoors in Stanley Park.

The show continues from mid-July to mid-August, weather permitting. It is especially fun with a picnic under a full moon. The **Vancouver East Cultural Centre**, at 1895 Venables Street (*tel: (604) 251 1363; www.vecc.bc.ca*), seems to specialise in avant-garde theatre, complemented by visual art exhibitions.

The **TheatreSports League** (call for times, or see *www.vtsl.com*) presents hilarious improvisations, often involving the audience, at the **Arts Club Revue Stage**, 1585 Johnston Street (*tel: (604) 738 7013*), from Wednesday to Saturday at 8pm. At the **Lafflines Comedy Club**, 26-4th Street, New Westminster (*tel: (604) 525 2262*), stand-up comics from all over the continent entertain from Tuesday to Saturday at 9pm. **Yuk Yuk's**, at 750 Pacific Boulevard

(*tel: (604) 687 LAFF*), also specialises in stand-up comedy.

The **Center in Vancouver for Performing Arts**, at 777 Homer Street (*tel: (604) 602 0616*), features a variety of live performances including drummers, magicians and solo acts like *Zamfir*.

Bard on the Beach
The **Bard on the Beach Theatre Society** (*tel: (604) 737 0625*) presents Shakespearean favourites in an open-ended candy-striped tent seating 300 people in Vanier Park adjacent to the Planetarium, on evenings in July and August. The setting is spectacular, as the stage has a backdrop of the North Shore mountains and sky coloured by the setting sun. Prices are reasonable, and reservations are recommended.

Open-air performances are always a big draw

Cinema

Vancouver has dozens of cinemas showing the latest feature films. Most are to be found downtown on the Granville Street Mall. The Park Royal Mall in West Vancouver has a multiplex; Metrotown Centre at Burnaby has two; and there are also several small cinemas in the Royal Centre Mall under the Hyatt Regency Hotel.

The **Pacific Cinématèque**, at 1131 Howe Street (*24-hour hotline: (604) 688 FILM*), is a non-profit, educational society dedicated to the enjoyment and study of film. Emphasis is on non-commercial classics such as *Bagdad Cafe* and Derek Jarman's *The Garden.*

The **Capitol 6 Cinemas** is at 820 Granville Street, downtown Vancouver (*tel: (604) 669 6000*). **Esplanade 6 Cinemas** is at 200 W. Esplanade, North Vancouver (*tel: (604) 983 2762*). **Station Square 7 Cinemas** is at Metrotown Centre, Burnaby (*tel: (604) 434 7711*).

The Ridge, at 3131 Arbutus Street (*tel: (604) 736 7006*), also features the classical and offbeat, serves delicious carrot cake and cappuccino, and has a kiddies' room.

The Famous Players Silver Screen Theatres run five cinemas: **SilverCity Metropolis** at Metrotown Centre, Burnaby (*tel: (604) 435 7474*); **SilverCity Riverport Road** at Richmond (*tel: (604) 277 5993*); **Cinemark Tinseltown** at 88 West Pender, downtown Vancouver (*tel: (604) 806 0799*); **IMAX Theatre-Canada Place** (*tel: (604) 682 IMAX*); and **Alcan Omnimax Theatre** at Science World (*tel: (604) 443 7443*). They are for more than just watching movies. They provide arcade games as well as a food court. They also have the IMAX theatre.

For more information, visit *www.famousplayers.com*

The annual **Vancouver International Film Festival** (*tel: (604) 685 0260; www.viff.org*), which takes place in early October, offers the best in current cinema from around the world.

Casinos

Gambling is highly regulated in Canada. Two of the major casinos, the **Great Canadian Casino** (*tel: (604) 303 1000; open: daily 10am–6am*) and the **Royal Diamond Casino** (*tel: (604) 899 1061; open: daily noon–4am*), abide by this. Dice are not permitted, so games are limited to roulette and blackjack. Non-alcoholic beverages and snacks are available. Fifty per cent of the proceeds go to local charities. The **Royal Diamond Casino** is at 750 Pacific Boulevard South. The **Great Canadian Casino** has four locations in the Lower Mainland. The closest one to downtown is in the Holiday Inn at 709 West Broadway.

Discos and clubs
Bacchus
The bar/lounge in the Wedgewood Hotel is the place to go if you want to rub shoulders with celebs in town for Vancouver's hot film production scene. *845 Hornby St. Tel: (604) 689 7777.*
Ginger Sixty-Two
A posh Fellini-esque ambience with a multitude of music styles. *1219 Granville St. Tel: (604) 688 5494.*
Shine
A trendy club that looks like *Clockwork Orange,* all white and glossy. *364 Water St, Gastown. Tel: (604) 408 4321.*

Voda

Attracts crowds of all ages to an intriguing interior of 1950s modernism. Waterfalls, rocks and hundreds of candles are a backdrop for Latin, R&B, funk and reggae.
In the Weston Grand Hotel, 783 Homer St. Tel: (604) 684 3003.

Richards on Richards

At this club, there are live bands for dancing to the tunes of the top 40, with recorded music between sets and video backdrops. Bar snacks are served.
1036 Richards St. Tel: (604) 687 6794.

Sonar

State-of-the-art techno club for the rave crowd, in the heart of historic Gastown.
66 Water St. Tel: (604) 683 6695.

The Purple Onion

Has a club and lounge atmosphere, and provides a great selection of Martinis.
15 Water St, Gastown. Tel: (604) 602 9442.

Bar None

Sounds of groove and house-funk. Popular in Vancouver.
1222 Hamilton St, downtown Vancouver. Tel: (604) 689 7000.

The Yale

Once voted the No 1 bar in town, it offers live music every day.
1300 Granville St. Tel: (604) 681 9253.

The Cellar Nightclub

Live house bands – BritRock and top-yo & hip hop.
1006 Granville St. Tel: (604) 605 4350.

Dinner plus

Blarney Stone

This lively Gastown restaurant features Irish and contemporary entertainment, starting at 7pm.
216 Carrall St. Tel: (604) 687 4322.

Shark Club Bar & Grill

This sports bar provides a warm ambience, created by a fireplace and rich mahogany surroundings. Sports fans enjoy the sports memorabilia, pool tables, dartboards and 30 television sets.
180 West Georgia St. Tel: (604) 687 4275.

Singing the blues

Children

Vancouver offers an abundance of attractions to entertain and educate youngsters. Some activities mentioned here are described in more detail in other parts of this book. For more suggestions, check Victoria Bushnell's *Kids Vancouver* or Fodor's *Vancouver with Kids*, and the Friday 'Family Fun' column in *The Vancouver Sun*, or try *www.findfamilyfun.com*

A kids-only market on Granville Island

Downtown
CN IMAX Theatre
A 400-seat cinema with a five-storey high wrap-around screen and superb sound facilities. Several different delightful short films and feature films offer scenic spectacles, outdoor adventure and even space travel, shown daily.
Canada Place. Tel: (604) 682 IMAX; www.imax.com/vancouver
Science World
Provides enough hands-on educational enjoyment for a whole day, and has a cafeteria on site for lunch. It is an ideal place to take children on a rainy day. The OMNIMAX cinema presents six shows daily. (*See pp68–9.*)
1455 Quebec St. Tel: (604) 443 7440; www.scienceworld.bc.ca
Stanley Park is a wonderful playground and children especially love the Miniature Railway (*tel: (604) 257 8531; www.city.vancouver.bc.ca/parks/parks/ stanley; open: 11am–4pm daily*), which rambles through a mini-wilderness, and the squirrels and raccoons which hang around Lost Lagoon. There are also 1-hr tours on an old-fashioned horse-drawn wagon through the 1,000-acre park (*tel: (604) 681 5115*). (*See pp70–71.*)

Aquarium
Kids enjoy touching the sea cucumbers, anemones, starfish and chitons (molluscs), and also love watching sea otters in a playful mood as they socialise underwater. (*See pp72–3.*)
Tel: (604) 685 3364; 24-hour info: (604) 659 FISH; www.vanaqua.org

For more water fun, there is the saltwater swimming pool – an enjoyable and safe option, which is supervised by lifeguards at Second Beach (*tel: (604) 257 8370*); and then there are the water parks on the Seawall near Lumberman's Arch and beside the fire engine playground near Pacific Avenue. Kids can burn up extra energy by cycling around the scenic 10-km (6-mile) Seawall.

Bicycle rentals are available near the Georgia Street entrance to the park.

Granville Island
Kids Only Market
Houses two dozen shops and other diversions. Special events are organised for weekends. On the south side outside is a Play Centre aimed at three- to five-year-olds.
1496 Cartwright St. Tel: (604) 689 8447. Open: daily 9am–6pm.

Weary parents can revive themselves with a cappuccino at The Cat's Meow, while children shower each other with big fire hoses attached to revolving fire hydrants at the supervised summertime **Water Park** in front.

Arts Umbrella

Two-week, day and half-day camps in summer are run for kids up to the age of 18. Classes include sculpture, dance, drama, painting, drawing and wood-carving. Reservations are advised. *1286 Cartwright St. Tel: (604) 681 5268; www.artsumbrella.com. 9am–3.30pm (with shorter days for pre-school children).*

Families can share outdoor fun with rental kayaks from Ecomarine, at 1668 Duranleau Street (*tel: (604) 689 7575*), and paddle around False Creek.

University of British Columbia

The **Museum of Anthropology** (*tel: (604) 822 5087; www.moa.ubc.ca*) lets children beat hanging drums and pull out dozens of drawers to examine native Indian toys, jewellery and clothing. Children enjoy feeding the fish at the Nitobe Japanese Gardens.

East Vancouver and Burnaby

Playland at the PNE (Pacific National Exhibition) Grounds

The rides are open from April to October. Attractions include the roller coaster, log-chute rides and the new 'Breakdance' and 'Gladiator' rides. Watching chickens hatch and cows calve during the Pacific National Exhibition in the last two weeks of August are especially interesting to city children. *Tel: (604) 253 2311; www.pne.ca*

Burnaby's Heritage Village and Carousel (*tel: (604) 293 6501; www.burnaby.ca*) is an open-air museum with costumed guides and old buildings recreating life between the 1890s and 1920s. **The Carousel** has 36 wooden horses, a chariot and four metal ponies.

North Vancouver

Maplewood Farm (*tel: (604) 929 5610; www.maplewoodfarm.bc.ca*) is a two-hectare park where children can get acquainted with domestic farm animals, have a pony ride, watch a milking demonstration and take a picnic by a meandering stream. **Capilano Suspension Bridge and Treetops** – safe but scary, the suspension bridge hangs 70m above a river and leads to a tranquil nature park trail through unspoilt rainforest. Treetops Adventure is the newest attraction here – a squirrel's-eye view from an elevated bridge hung between magnificent Douglas fir trees. *Tel: (604) 985 7474.*

Storyeum is a dramatised romp through BC's history using multimedia techniques. *142 Water St, Gastown. Tel: (604) 687 8142, toll free (800) 687 8142; www.storyeum.com*

New Westminster

It is well worth overcoming any feelings of claustrophobia to visit the remarkable **Russian Submarine** at the waterfront on New Westminster Quay. *Tel: (604) 520 3881. Open: daily 9.30am–6.30pm; www.westminsterquay.com*

S p o r t   a n d   l e i s u r e

Vancouver is an absolute mecca for sports lovers. The long days of summer are great for golf and tennis; the beaches and sea breezes appeal to swimmers and sailors; there are lots of trails for cyclists and hikers; and local fresh and salt waters teem with life for eager anglers and divers. Come June, Vancouver hosts the Alcan Dragon Boat Festival, North America's longest-running event of its kind (*www.adbf.com*), and in winter skiers head for the mountains.

Summer sunshine is great for golfing

LAND SPORTS
Bowling
Vancouver has 20 bowling alleys, some five-pin, some ten-pin. Check the *Yellow Pages* for details of opening times.

Bungee jumping
The sport that New Zealand made famous came quickly to BC. You can jump off a bridge at the Bungy Zone, about a 15-minute drive south of Nanaimo (*tel: (604) 753 JUMP*), or call Playland (*tel: (604) 253 2311*) and leap from a 75-m (246-foot) crane for the longest step of your life (summer only).

Caving
There are about 2,000 caves in BC, mostly on Vancouver Island, all in original condition, with no walkways. Only 600 of them have been charted.

Popular caves for exploring include the Black Hole (situated in virgin rainforest), the Horne Lake Caves, Paradise Lost and the Artlish River Cave. Contact *www.cancaver.ca* for information on cave tour operators.

Cycling
The Stanley Park Seawall (*see pp74–5*) provides the perfect path for an hour of urban cycling. The paved trail following the SkyTrain route from Main St station to New Westminster is also relatively flat and passes 32 parks and playgrounds. Spokes Bicycle Rentals (*tel: (604) 688 5141*) and other downtown operations rent bicycles by the hour or by the day.

Golfing
The province's 160 golf courses include 17 in Vancouver, all open to the public. A letter of introduction from your home club provides entry to private courses. Several par-three courses are scattered throughout the city. Langara Golf Course at 6706 Alberta Street (*tel: (604) 713 1816*) is one of the best in BC; another is the McCleery Golf Course in South Vancouver at 7188 MacDonald Street (*tel: (604) 251 8181*).

Hiking and walking
Most major parks in and around Vancouver have well-marked circuits for

scenic wilderness hikes and walks. The Stanley Park Seawall is the best walk close to downtown (*see pp74–5*). Lynn Canyon is an equally spectacular, but a cheaper and quieter, alternative to Capilano (and it has its own suspension bridge). Lynn Canyon Ecology Centre on the North Shore (*tel: (604) 981 3103*) provides films and summer nature programmes about the environment.

Horse riding

Urban equestrians enjoy the trails at Langley 204 Stables at 543–204th Street (*tel: (604) 533 7978*), which offers 18km (11 miles) of trails on good-quality horses. Riders with more time may want to rough it with wranglers on the range, such as the one at Ashcroft known as the Sundance Guest Ranch (*tel: (604) 453 2422 or toll free (800) 553 3533; www.sundanceguestranch.com*).

Paragliding

'Flight-seeing' is an exhilarating way to view the spectacular BC scenery for those who have the nerve. Mount Seven in the Rockies is a site of international competitions for paragliding and hang-gliding, but for a beginner's introduction to the sport Grouse Mountain is ideal. Flights in tandem with a professional pilot are available daily between March and September (weather permitting). Call First Flight Paragliding (*tel: (604) 980 9311; www.grousemountain.com*).

Rock climbing

In a region with so many mountains, rock climbing is almost an instinct. Learners practise in Lighthouse Park in West Vancouver on cliffs overhanging

the water, and then move on to tough mountain challenges. **Cliffhanger Indoor Rock Climbing Centre** (*tel: (604) 874 2400*) has nearly 1,000sq m of walls to climb. **Playland** (*tel: (604) 253 2311*) offers a 12-m (39-foot) outdoor climbing wall in the Extreme Action Zone of the grounds. Contact the Federation of Mountain Clubs of BC (*tel: (604) 873 6096; www.mountainclubs.bc.ca*).

Skiing

Vancouver's North Shore has three ski areas within a half-hour drive of the city centre. The nearest is Grouse Mountain (1,250m/4,101 feet), where in good weather skiers enjoy spectacular views down to the city centre and across Georgia Strait to the Gulf Islands and Vancouver Island.

Cypress Bowl to the west and Mount Seymour to the east also offer nordic skiing. Cypress and Grouse are lit for evening skiing until 10pm. All three mountains have equipment rentals and restaurants. For more information, visit *www.skihills.com*

Tennis

More than 200 public courts, scattered throughout the city, are free and operate on a first come, first serve basis. Stanley Park charges a court fee in summer.

Cyclists on Mayne Island

Skiing

BC is one of Canada's top ski playgrounds. The combination of the moderate climate with the proximity of Vancouver airport to good ski facilities, comfortable accommodation and challenging terrain appeals to skiers from around the globe.

When moist, cold air from the Pacific meets the coastal mountains, the result is big flakes of snow which pack the mountain peaks and slopes.

The three North Shore mountains, Cypress, Grouse and Seymour – all within a half-hour drive from Vancouver city centre – offer spectacular sea and city vistas, along with good ski facilities open day and evening from November to April when the snows permit.

Japanese skiers have named Whistler/Blackcomb, fast becoming a subject for superlatives all over the world, their favourite ski area, leaving Vail, Chamonix and Zermatt in the shadows. Here, a two-hour drive north from Vancouver, high-speed quad chairs and other lifts run up spectacular slopes to a variety of gentle runs for novices, alpine chutes, glades, groomed runs, moguls and vast areas of backcountry for skilled skiers.

Hemlock, in the Fraser Valley, also accommodates overnight guests at its cosy alpine village, and offers 30km (19 miles) of groomed trails. Manning Park Resort is a small, family-style ski area at the northern end of the Cascades.

Nordic skiing along trails in the Lower Mainland presents a range of exciting challenges. The 16km (10 miles) of hilly tracks and packed trails at Hollyburn Ridge on Cypress Mountain are open all day and evening until 10pm. The Diamond Head area in Garibaldi Park has high glaciers, with an overnight hut available at Elfin Lakes. The Hemlock Valley loop comprises 30km (19 miles) of groomed trails, good for both cross-country and telemark skiing.

Other downhill and nordic ski areas are scattered throughout the BC interior. For the adventurous, there is heli-skiing in the Bugaboos and at Tyax, north of Whistler, and there is snowcat skiing in the Selkirk Mountains.

SOME POPULAR SKI RESORTS

Vancouver

Cypress Mountain Ski Area. *Tel: (604) 419 SNOW; www.cypressmountain.com*
Grouse Mountain. *Tel: (604) 980 9311 or (604) 986 6262; www.grousemountain.com*
Mount Seymour Ski Resort. *Tel: (604) 986 2261; www.mountseymour.com*

British Columbia

Whistler/Blackcomb, Whistler. *Tel: (604) 932 3434; www.whistler-blackcomb.com*
Silver Star Mountain Ski Resort, Vernon. *Tel: (250) 542 0224; www.skisilverstar.com*
Big White Ski Resort, Kelowna. *Tel: (250) 765 3101; www.bigwhite.com*

WATER SPORTS

Vancouver has water on three sides, and BC has more than 7,000km of coastline, 11,000 rivers and creeks, 6,000 lakes, 30 coastal marine parks and countless tidal inlets, offering unmatched opportunities for adventure. (*See* Getting Away, *pp127–31.*)

Canoeing

A number of companies specialise in outdoor adventures. They can arrange canoeing trips for half a day or week-long excursions with full catering. Lotus Land Tours (*tel: (604) 684 4922 or 800 528 3531 toll free; www.vancouvernatureadventures.com*) offer a half-day nature adventure with free pick-up in Vancouver.

Fishing

A fishing licence (saltwater or freshwater, or both), sold in major downtown department stores and in sporting goods shops, is essential. The interior season extends from May to October, while coastal waters may operate year-round.

Watch the expert boatracers skim over the waters

Numerous rivers and lakes contain trout and salmon. Arctic grayling, pike and walleye inhabit northern waters, while the boundary areas contain smallmouth bass and yellow perch. Sturgeon live in the Fraser and Columbia rivers and bass are found on Vancouver Island.

Spring or chinook salmon and coho are the most popular saltwater catches, although some anglers prefer the challenges of sockeye, pink and chum salmon. Coastal waters also harbour halibut, flounder, sole, red snapper, perch, greenling, ling cod and the spotted sea-run cut-throat trout. Such shellfish as abalone, clams, oysters, crabs, mussels, scallops, shrimps and prawns also inhabit these waters. Restrictions concerning size and species are outlined in the *BC Tidal Waters Sport Fishing Guide.*

You can either take a fishing charter, which will look after everything, or you can rent a motorboat. Canadian Coho Charters (*tel: (604) 435 7333*) at 4152 Penticton Street, Vancouver and Sewell's Marina in Horseshoe Bay (*tel: (604) 921 3474*) offer both charters and bareboat rentals.

Kayaking

Ecomarine at 1668 Duranleau St (*tel: (604) 689 7575; www.ecomarine.com*), on Granville Island, rents kayaks all year round.

A two-hour rental allows ample time to glide along the quiet waters of False Creek past the market deck, the floating houseboat homes, Science World and the residential community along the south shore. Both one- and two-seater kayaks are available. Talasay Tours has kayaking, canoeing, hiking and snowshoeing tours led by Candace Campo, a First Nations guide with a rich knowledge of local flora and fauna and native legends (*tel: (604) 628 8555, toll free (800) 605 4643; www.talaysaytours.com*).

Batstar Adventure Tours have well-organised, relaxed, fun kayaking tours into the wilderness of Vancouver Island's Broken Islands group using top-of-the-line equipment, luxury tents and serving gourmet food (*tel: tollfree (877) 449 1230; www.batstar.com*).

Motor boating

Canada's largest fleet of self-drive rental boats is moored in Horseshoe Bay, 17km (10$^1/_2$ miles) northwest of downtown. Here, Sewell's Marina (*tel: (604) 921 3474; www.sewellsmarina.com*) rents boats by the hour and longer – a great way to explore the coastline and nearby islands.

River rafting

In this exhilarating social sport, a dozen or so novices and a couple of expert guides challenge the white water. Such Vancouver companies as Hyak Wilderness Adventures (*tel: (604) 734 8622, toll free (800) 663 7238; www.hyak.com*) offer trips varying from a heart-thumping afternoon ride to six-day trips through the stunning scenery of BC's most exciting rivers.

Scuba diving

BC's underwater world is a submarine jungle of graceful giant anemones, towering sea-whips, gorgonian corals and other marine life.

Howe Sound is one of the most popular diving areas, and at Porteau Cove, on its eastern shore, a Provincial Marine Park has been established, with old ship hulls forming an artificial reef.

Though the surface waters are reasonably warm, the temperature below the thermocline persists at about 10°C, so divers will need a 6mm neoprene wet suit or, even better, a custom dry suit.

Equipment is available for hire from a number of dive shops, including Divers World, at 1695 West 4th Avenue (*tel: (604) 732 1344; www.bcdive.com*). The International Diving Centre at 2572 Arbutus St. (*tel: (604) 736 2541; www.diveidc.com*) organises day, weekend or longer trips.

Swimming

English Bay beaches offer good swimming in summer, but seekers of solitude may prefer Savary Island and Desolation Sound further north, where the waters are just as warm.

The freshwater pool at Second Beach in Stanley Park and Kits pool (Vancouver's only saltwater pool) at 2305 Cornwall (*tel: (604) 731 0011*) are open from May to September.

Indoor pools at the University of British Columbia (UBC) Aquatic Centre at 6121 University Boulevard (*tel: (604) 822 4522*), the Vancouver Aquatic Centre at 1050 Beach Avenue (*tel: (604) 665 3424*) and the YMCA at 955 Burrand downtown (*tel: (604) 689 YMCA; www.vanymca.ca*) are open day and evening throughout the year. Check out *www.vancouverparks.ca* for a complete list of city beaches and pools.

A killer whale at close quarters

SPECTATOR SPORTS
Whale watching

Watching these great mammals of the Pacific is a favourite spectator sport of both residents and visitors. Johnstone Strait, between Vancouver Island and the mainland, is home to the world's largest concentration of killer whales that can be seen on a daily basis.

These sheltered waters, about 400km (249 miles) northwest of Vancouver, are home to 12 pods, totalling approximately 135 killer whales. When conditions permit, you can listen with a hydrophone to orcas emitting their famous songs and clicks. The total killer whale population of BC is around 300. The whales have a low birthrate and a low mortality rate. The males may live for up to 50 years, while the females may live twice as long. Johnstone Strait is also home for many sea birds and bald eagles, salmon, seals, sea lions, porpoises, minke whales, humpback whales, harbour seals and Pacific white-sided dolphins.

Off the west coast of Vancouver Island, spring is the time to see the big grey whales migrating from Baja

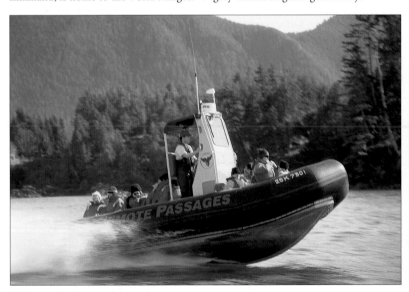

Whale watching is a popular excursion

The Vancouver Canucks take on the Phoenix Coyotes

California to Alaska. Several companies, such as **Orca Spirit Adventures** (*tel: 1 (888) 672 ORCA*), provide watching tours. Bring binoculars. **Vancouver Whale Watch** in Richmond is the only whale-watching outfit on the lower mainland (*tel: (604) 274 9565; www.vancouverwhalewatch.com*).

Team sports

For those who enjoy the roar of the crowd, there are the BC Lions (*tel: (604) 589 ROAR*) who play home games in the Canadian Football League at BC Place Stadium (777 Pacific Boulevard); the Vancouver Canadians AAA baseball team – one step below major league standard – (*tel: (604) 872 5232; www.canadiansbaseball.com*), who perform at Nat Bailey Stadium (33rd Ave, Ontario St, adjacent to Queen Elizabeth Park); the Vancouver Whitecaps soccer team (*tel: (604) 669 9283 WAVE;* Swangard Stadium, in Burnaby); and, in winter, the Vancouver Canucks ice hockey team who compete in the National Hockey League at GM Place downtown. Information on seasons, game times, venues and tickets is available from the Travel InfoCentre (*tel: (604) 683 2000*).

Horse racing

Horse racing takes place from mid-April to the end of November at Vancouver's Hastings Racecourse (*tel: (604) 254 1631, toll free (800) 677 7702; www.hastingspark.com*). Betting diners can watch the races on closed-circuit television, but the view of Mount Seymour across Burrard Inlet from the stands is so spectacular that it would be a shame to miss it.

Food and drink

East and West meet in Vancouver in an amazing variety of restaurants, some Oriental, some European, some African, some North American, and others which artfully combine and innovate to create new cuisines.

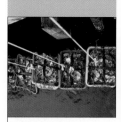

Oysters, fresh from the ocean

Fine foods and wines are often found in Vancouver at lower prices than in Europe. Dinner usually costs more than lunch for the same menu, and breakfast is the bargain of the day. Many restaurants are closed on Monday. Except for fast-food places, reservations are recommended for lunch during the week and for dinner on Friday and Saturday evenings. Most restaurants accept major credit cards. Restaurants do not add a service charge, so a tip of between 10 and 20 per cent is welcome.

Restaurants listed are categorised according to price per person for a full-course meal, not including alcohol.

★   under C$10
★★   between
        C$10–20
★★★   between
        C$20–35
★★★★ over C$35

BREAKFAST AND BRUNCH

Elbow Room Cafe ★★
Plastered with clippings and photos of the rich and famous, and vibrates with the energy of the two owners.
560 Davie St. Tel: (604) 685 3628.

Joe's Grill ★★★
Highly recommended for its delicious breakfasts.
2061 West 4th Ave in Kitsilano. Tel: (604) 736 658.

Sophie's Cosmic Cafe ★
A great place to take kids for breakfast or otherwise.
*2095 W. Fourth Ave.
Tel: (604) 732 6810.*

Sunshine Diner ★★
Top-notch food (especially breakfast, eggs and waffles), fast service.
*2756 W Broadway.
Tel: (604) 733 7717.*

CHINESE RESTAURANTS

Floata Seafood Restaurant ★★★
The biggest Chinese banquet restaurant in the heart of Vancouver's Chinatown.
*400–180 Keefer St.
Tel: (604) 602 0368.*

Hon's Wun-Tun House ★★
A popular place for Cantonese cuisine.
*1339 Robson St.
Tel: (604) 685 0871.*

The Pink Pearl ★★★
The city's best Cantonese restaurant.
*1132 East Hastings St.
Tel: (604) 253 4316.*

Shao Lin Noodle Restaurant ★
Inexpensive but yummy noodle dishes in a busy atmosphere.
*548 W Broadway.
Tel: (604) 873 1816.*

Sun Sui Wah ★★
Good dim sum and congee, and very popular.
*3888 Main St.
Tel: (604) 872 8822.*

JAPANESE RESTAURANTS

Kamei Royale ★★★★
There is always a special new addition to the long-

time favourite menu.
1030 W Georgia St.
Tel: (604) 687 8588.
Matsubishi ★★★★
An award-winning
restaurant where live
seafood is cooked to
order at your tableside.
*2nd floor, 755 Burrard St
(entrance on Alberni St).*
Tel: (604) 669 3838.
Raku ★★★★
Tasty and unusual
Japanese dishes.
4422 W 10th.
Tel: (604) 222 8188.
Tanpopo ★★
One of Vancouver's
first all-you-can-eat
sushi spots and still

serving great sashimi.
Frenzied atmosphere
but sushi fanatics
love it.
1122 Denman St.
Tel: (604) 681 7777.
**Tojo Japanese
Restaurant ★★★★**
One of the best in North
America.
777 W Broadway.
Tel: (604) 872 8050.
Yoshi's on Denman ★★★
Rated by Vancouver
Magazine as one of the
city's best. Fresh seafood,
great ambience and patio
dining.
689 Denman St.
Tel: (604) 738 8226.

INDIAN RESTAURANTS
Heaven and Earth ★★★
Authentic Indian
cuisine, sitar music
and a relaxed
atmosphere.
1754 W 4th Ave.
Tel: (604) 732 5313.
Tandoori King ★★★
A favourite among the
city's food specialists.
689 E 65th St.
Tel: (604) 327 8900.

THAI RESTAURANTS
Montri-Thai ★★
City restaurateurs like to
dine here.
3629 W Broadway.
Tel: (604) 738 9888.

Good restaurants and cafés can be found throughout Vancouver

Dim sum brunch

A Sunday-morning crowd slowly moves up a staircase to the second floor, to a cultural experience and fast food at its finest. This is Ming's in Vancouver's Chinatown, one of the biggest and best *dim sum* restaurants in town.

A dish of small steamed or fried savoury dumplings containing various fillings, *dim sum* means 'a little bit of heart' in Cantonese, and both Cantonese and other Canadians are eating to their hearts' delight. It is a lively and happy occasion and often a family affair.

Dim sum regulars arrive early and sit near the kitchen for the first choice of freshest food. A procession of little carts, carrying stacks of steaming bamboo baskets and stainless steel containers filled with dozens of different delights, are wheeled among the tables, where hundreds of people are enjoying some of the more than 50 listed delicacies.

Popular *dim sum* includes *ha gow*, a thin rice dough wrapped around bits of prawns and bamboo shoots and steamed; *cha siu bao*, dumpling-like buns filled with barbecued pork; and sticky rice wrapped in lotus leaves.

Dim sum diners can eat a little, or a lot, and pay accordingly. Each portion usually contains two or three bite-sized pieces. The complimentary green jasmine tea, or the robust black *bo lei*,

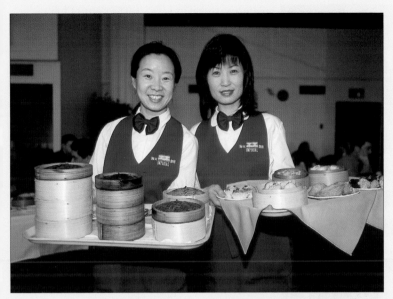

goes well with *dim sum*. When the teapot is empty, simply lift the lid and the waiter quickly refills it. To say thank you, tap your first two fingers on the table. Chinese and local beer go well with *dim sum*.

Dim sum restaurants are not renowned for décor. Arrive early and the place looks bleak. Arrive later, and the animated eaters, the ebony-eyed waitresses and the choreography of the carts in the moveable feast create a splendid scenario. And the noise is a joyful one.

Dim sum remains an all-time favourite when eating out in Chinatown

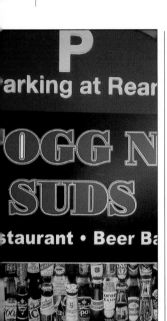
Enjoying a beer at Fogg n' Suds

EUROPEAN RESTAURANTS

The Chef and Carpenter ★★★★
A top chef creates fine French food here.
1745 Robson St.
Tel: (604) 687 2700.

Le Gavroche ★★★★
In the cosy and charming upstairs of an old house (the two window tables offer a great harbour view), Le Gavroche has received several awards for fine cuisine, which ranges from classic European dishes to *mahi mahi* and smoked duck.
1616 Alberni St.
Tel: (604) 685 3924.

Lumiere ★★★
French cuisine can be enjoyed inside or on the patio in fine weather. Valet parking is a bonus.
2551 W Broadway.
Tel: (604) 739 8185.

Marcello's ★★
Looks more expensive than it is. Great Italian comfort food.
1404 Commercial Drive.
Tel: (604) 215 7760.

Maria's Taverna ★★
People in the food business come here for Greek food.
2324 W 4th Ave.
Tel: (604) 731 4722.

Omitsky Kosher Foods ★
Great Hebrew food, from corned beef to matzoh ball soup.
5866 Cambie St.
Tel: (604) 321 1818.

Villa del Lupo ★★★
Timeless Italian cuisine in a Mediterranean-style setting.
869 Hamilton St.
Tel: (604) 688 7436.

FAST FOOD

A&W ★
A favourite with younger children.
Sinclair Centre.
Tel: (604) 687 4186.

The Cactus Club ★★
Famous for Mexican fajitas and burgers.
1136 Robson St.
Tel: (604) 687 3278.

C-Lover's Fish & Chips ★
Tempura-like batter and great chips.
1660 Pemberton Ave.
Tel: (604) 980 9993.

Flying Wedge Pizza ★★
You pay a bit more, but great pizza. Numerous outlets in the city, but this one is in Vancouver's beautiful library.
207–345 Robson St.
Tel: (604) 689 7078.

Fogg n' Suds Restaurant ★
Fun and casual, with an international menu.
1323 Robson St.
Tel: (604) 683 2337.

Food Fair ★
There is fast food from many countries in this mall food area.
Pacific Centre, Howe and Dunsmuir.

The Noodle Express ★★
Among the best of the Japanese sushi and noodle houses.
747 Thurlow St.
Tel: (604) 669 1234.

The Old Spaghetti Factory ★★
Good family fare – a great place to take children.
53 Water St, Gastown.
Tel: (604) 684 1288.

Red Robin ★★
Burgers and fries with
some Mexican food.
803 Thurlow St.
Tel: (604) 662 8288.

White Spot ★
A Vancouver legend,
especially burgers.
Various outlets.
580 W Georgia St.
Tel: (604) 662 3066.

FISH RESTAURANTS

C ★★★
Dubbed Vancouver's most
innovative and creative
seafood restaurant – try
the octopus-wrapped
scallops or soft-shell crab.
2–1600 Howe St.
Tel: (604) 681 1164.

Cannery Seafood House
★★★★
Down on the docks and
elegantly rustic, the views
here vie with the freshest
fish.
2205 Commissioner St.
Tel: (604) 254 9606

The Fish House ★★★★
Exceptional seafood and
fresh oyster bar, with
sunny patios overlooking
English Bay.
8901 Stanley Park Drive.
Tel: (604) 681 7275.

PLACES TO TALK

**Bacchus Restaurant
& Lounge** ★★★★
The place in town
for mood lighting,
quiet conversation
and a good chance of
spotting well-known
celebrities.
845 Hornby St.
Tel: (604) 689 7777.

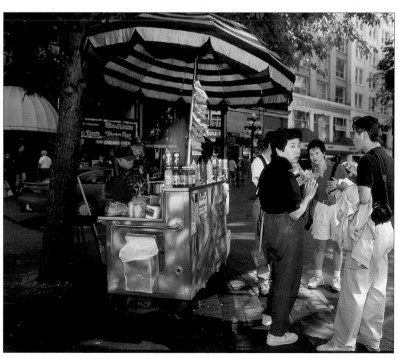

Pick up a hot dog at one of the many wagons

La Bodega ★★
Tasty *tapas* here include the best fried chicken in town, and patrons love the informal Spanish atmosphere.
1277 Howe St.
Tel: (604) 684 8814/5.

Hotel Vancouver Lounge ★★
One of the city's great meeting places.
900 W Georgia St.
Tel: (604) 684 3131.

Joe Fortes ★★★
Haunt of yuppies, and a good place for people-watching.
777 Thurlow St.
Tel: (604) 669 1940.

Seawall Bar and Bistro ★★★
A cosy place in West Coast nautical style that is comfortable even when packed.

Bayshore Hotel, 1601 W Georgia St.
Tel: (604) 682 3377.

Pan Pacific Lobby Lounge ★★★
Spectacular views of the Alaska cruise ships and the harbour.
999 Canada Place.
Tel: (604) 662 8111.

Sylvia Hotel Bar ★★
The best place to watch the sun set over English Bay.
Beach and Gilford.
Tel: (604) 681 9321.

Umberto Al Porto ★★★
This good Italian restaurant is also the home of Umberto's Wine Club.
321 Water St, Gastown.
Tel: (604) 683 8376.

Zin ★★★
Patrons here enjoy great food, live music and wickered comfort, while

looking out on Robson Street.
Pacific Palisades Hotel, 1277 Robson St.
Tel: (604) 408 1700;

VEGETARIAN FOOD
Bejuiced Vegetarian Cuisine ★★
Everything made from scratch.
1958 W 4th Ave.
Tel: (604) 730 9906.

Bodhi Vegetarian ★★★
Provides good, no-meat meals.
3932 Fraser.
Tel: (604) 873 3848.

Greens and Gourmet ★★★★
Soft new-age music, bright greenery-filled rooms and fine vegetarian cuisine.
2582 W Broadway.
Tel: (604) 737 7373.

Pick up a snack at Granville Island market

Naam Restaurant ★★
A famous 24-hour
vegetarian restaurant
with a wood fireplace
and heated patio.
2724 W 4th Ave.
Tel: (604) 738 7151.

**Woodlands Natural
Foods** ★★
A good menu of
vegetarian food here; you
can select from the buffet
and pay by weight.
2582 W Broadway.
Tel: (604) 733 5411.

WEST COAST
Bishop's ★★★★
Consistently praised for its
impeccable service,
Bishop's also has an
extensive cellar with a good
range of Californian and
Pacific Northwest wines.
2183 W 4th Ave.
Tel: (604) 738 2025.
**Bud's Halibut and
Chips** ★★
Not surprisingly, the
halibut here is
particularly good.
1007 Denman St.
Tel: (604) 683 0661.
Café Madeleine ★★
No madeleines on the
menu, but the sandwiches
are excellent; a favourite
with University of British
Columbia students.
3761 W 10th Ave.
Tel: (604) 224 5558.

Asian cuisine is a staple in BC

Delilah's ★★★
The old railroad-style
menus here offer a set-
price, two-course and
five-course dinner.
1789 Comox St.
Tel: (604) 687 3424.
Liliget Feast House ★★★
This is Vancouver's only
restaurant specialising in
the food of the native
Indian people. It is in a
simulated Indian
longhouse with gravelled
walkways and sunken
tables. The chef works at
an open grill over an
alderwood fire, and his
specialities include
oolichan, bannock bread,
caribou, salmon cheeks
and whipped soap berries.
1724 Davie St.
Tel: (604) 681 7044.
**Observatory
Restaurant** ★★★★
The magnificent views
from the summit, and the

inclusive Skyride trip up
the mountain, are just
two good reasons to dine
at the Grouse Nest. The
superbly cooked West
Coast specialities would
be worth doing the
'Grouse Grind' for.
*Grouse Mountain, 6400
Nancy Greene Way, N
Vancouver.*
Tel: (604) 980 9311.
The Only Café ★★
The 'only' theme is
carried on beyond the
name of this restaurant –
it only serves fish, only
perfect, and is the only
restaurant in town
without a washroom!
20 E Hastings St.
Tel: (604) 681 6546.
Raincity Grill ★★★★
A 'buy local, eat seasonal'
restaurant. This is a gem.
Always makes 'best' lists.
1193 Denman St.
Tel: (604) 685 7337.

The Raintree ★★★

Local specialities here include sorrel soup, wild greens with edible flowers, salmon and Okanagan apple pie.
375 Water St.
Tel: (604) 688 5570.

The Salmon House on the Hill ★★★

Salmon is barbecued over alderwood here, and the view over the city is spectacular.
2229 Folkstone Way.
Tel: (604) 926 3212.

West ★★★★

Named the best restaurant in Vancouver, West takes French food and gives it a mouthwatering West Coast twist!
2881 Granville St.
Tel: (604) 738 8938.

VICTORIA

Camille's ★★★★

Good seasonal local food in the perfect spot for a romantic dinner.
45 Bastion Square.
Tel: (250) 381 3433.

Darb's Place ★

Rated as one of the best places to get traditional British fish and chips.
310 St. Lawrence Square
Tel: (250) 384 6515.

J+J Wonton Noodle House ★★

A local favourite, the best noodles and fresh

seafood.
1012 Fort St.
Tel: (250) 383 0680.

Millos ★★★

Look for a blue and white windmill downtown for great Greek food and entertainment.
716 Burdett Ave.
Tel: (250) 382 4422.

Ottavio Italian Bakery & Delicatessen ★★

Over 200 wonderful artisan cheeses and an assortment of Italian food products, this small eatery is a true insider's secret.
2272 Oak Bay Ave.
Tel: (250) 592 4080.

Spinnaker's Brew Pub ★★

Great beers accompany average food in this informal pub.
308 Catherine St, Victoria West.
Tel: (250) 384 6613.

Il Terrazzo ★★★★

About as good as Northern Italian cuisine comes, with meals alfresco all year round by outdoor fireplaces if you choose.
555 Johnson St.
Tel: (250) 361 0028.

PUBS

There are few traditional British-style pubs in BC, probably because the province is too young, the population too transitory

and the drinking laws too strict. Until the BC government first permitted neighbourhood pubs in the late 1960s, most public drinking was confined to hotels and restaurants. The pubs that do exist today include some good ones attached to local breweries. Good local brews, usually on tap, come from the Steamworks Brewing Company, Yaletown Brewing Company, Granville Island Brewery and Whistler lagers. There is also the Horseshoe Bay brewery, which, when it opened in 1981, was the first cottage brewery built in Canada in 50 years, and also produces a more than palatable ale.

Generally speaking, the further the watering hole from the big city, the friendlier the staff and the clientele.

Fanny Bay Inn

This is one of the oldest pubs, built in 1938, and famous for its oysters, barbecued beef, pork and lamb, and staff who make visitors feel like locals.
4480 S Island Road, near Courtenay, Vancouver Island.
Tel: (250) 335 2323.

The Jolly Taxpayer Pub
The sense of humour in this pub's name is reflected in the fun atmosphere inside.
828 W Hastings St.
Tel: (604) 681 3574.

Kingston Taphouse & Grille
Contemporary urban pub and restaurant with six unique rooms in the heart of Vancouver.

755 Richards St.
Tel: (604) 681 7011.

Moose's Down Under Restaurant
This Australian-style pub is open for breakfast, lunch and dinner, and offers exceptional value.
830 West Pender St.
Tel: (604) 683 3300.

Steamworks Brewing Company
A lovely old heritage

building is the location of this pub, with good beer and home-made food.
375 Water St, Gastown.
Tel: (604) 689 2739.

Yaletown Brewing Company
Right in the heart of trendy Yaletown. Pizzas are made in a traditional wood oven.
1111 Mainland St.
Tel: (604) 681 BREW.

BC wines now get rave reviews from all over the world

Hotels and accommodation

Accommodation in BC ranges from rustic campsites to sybaritic suites with all amenities. Reservations are recommended, especially during the crowded days of summer. The Travel InfoCentre (HelloBC), at 200 Burrard Street, operates a hotel reservation service (*tel: (604) 663 6000*). Current hotel tax is 17 per cent, but 7 per cent is refundable to non-Canadians when total tax paid comes to C$100. HelloBC will provide free tourism information and the comprehensive *BC Accommodations Guide.*

The Fairmont Hotel is known for its excellent service

De luxe hotels

Two of Canada's five-diamond CAA/AAA hotels are in Vancouver: the **Four Seasons** (*tel: (604) 689 9333; www.fourseasons.com*) and **Sutton Place** (*tel: (604) 682 5511; www.vancouver. suttonplace.com*). The Four Seasons sits atop the Pacific Centre's underground mall of 200 shops; Sutton Place also manages the spacious apartments in **La Grande Residence** next door (minimum stay one month).

Most luxury hotels have pools, spas, restaurants, 24-hour room service and valet parking, and most are wheelchair-accessible. Rates run from C$290 per room per night. De luxe downtown hotels include the **Fairmont Hotel Vancouver** (*tel: (604) 684 3131; www.fairmont.com*), a city landmark which has undergone a C$10 million renovation, plus a brand new spa; the **Hyatt Regency** (*tel: (604) 683 1234; www.vancouver.hyatt.com*) above the Royal Centre Mall; the sparkling **Pan Pacific** (*tel: (604) 662 8111; www.panpac.com*), overlooking the harbour; the **Renaissance** (*tel: (604) 689 9211; www.renaissancevancouver.com*), with its revolving restaurant; the **Westin Bayshore and Marina** (*tel: (604) 682 3377; www.westinbayshore.com*), Vancouver's only downtown resort hotel; and the **Fairmont Waterfront Centre Hotel** (*tel: (604) 691 1991; www.fairmont.com*) behind the Pan Pacific.

Moderately priced hotels

These hotels, priced from about C$140 for a double room, offer comfortable and clean accommodation.

Moderately priced hotels include the **Barclay Hotel** (*tel: (604) 688 8850; www.barclayhotel.com*), an 85-room European-style establishment with a licensed lounge and restaurant; the **Sandman Hotel** (*tel: (604) 681 2211, toll free (800) Sandman; www.sandmanhotels.com*), within walking distance of Robson Street, Chinatown and Gastown; the **Oceanside Apartment Hotel** (*tel: (604) 682 5641, toll free (877) 506 2326; www.oceanside-hotel.com*), on English Bay, two blocks from Stanley Park; the **Riviera Hotel** (*tel: (604) 685 1301, toll free (888) 699 5222; www.vancouver-bc.com/rivierahotel*) on Robson St, which offers 40 suites with balconies; the **Sunset Inn** (*tel: (604) 688 2474, toll free (800) 786 1997; www.sunsetinn.com*), which has 50 suites with kitchens (weekly and monthly rates available); and the **Best Western Château** (*tel: (604) 669 7070, toll free (800) 663 7070; www.bwcg.com*), on Granville Street, mostly suite accommodation close to all downtown attractions. Also check out the **Rosellen Suites** at Stanley Park (*tel: (604) 689 4807, (888) 317 6648; www.rosellensuites.com*) and the **Victorian Hotel** (*tel: (604) 681 6369; fax: (604) 681 8776; www.victorianhotel.ca*).

Cost-cutters

Several reasonably priced hotels (from about C$75 for a double room) are found throughout the downtown area. **Shaughnessy Village** (*tel: (604) 736 5511; www.shaughnessyvillage.com*) rooms are small but the hotel has amenities galore: free health club and current 24-hr movies; pool, miniature golf, billiards and more. **The Kingston Hotel** (*tel: (604) 684 9024; www.kingstonhotelvancouver.com*) offers a complimentary breakfast and a 10 per cent discount for senior citizens and students. The **YMCA** (*tel: (604) 681 0221; www.vanymca.org*) offers good bargains for single people and couples.

Pillow Suites (*tel: (604) 879 8977; www.pillow.net*) offer homely and neat suites with fully equipped kitchen, washers and dryers.

The **Vancouver Youth Hostel** (*tel: (604) 684 4565; www.hihostels.bc.ca*) is located in the heart of Vancouver's lively West End within minutes of shops, restaurants and beaches. Heaps of amenities including a fully equipped kitchen.

The **University of British Columbia** (*tel: (604) 822 1000; www.pacificspirithostel.com*) and **Simon Fraser University** (*tel: (604) 291 4503; www.sfu.ca/conference-accommodation*) offer summer housing from May through to August. Both have single rooms with shared bath, and UBC also has several studio and one-bed suites.

Bed-and-breakfast

Greater Vancouver has numerous bed-and-breakfast establishments, some luxurious, some spartan. When booking, enquire whether smoking is permitted and credit cards are accepted. To find a B&B, check Western Canada Bed & Breakfast Innkeepers Association (*www.wcbbia.com*) or call HelloBC (*tel: (604) 663 6000*).

Campsites

Several campsites are scattered throughout the city, but the **Capilano RV Park** (*tel: (604) 987 4722; fax: (604) 987 2015; www.capilanorvpark.com*) in North Vancouver has the most dramatic setting. There are sites for 190 motorhomes and 10 tents. The park has 24-hour-a-day supervision, a TV lounge, a Jacuzzi and a swimming pool.

Practical guide

Arriving
Entry formalities
Requirements include a valid full
passport (except for Americans) and a
return or onward ticket, together with
evidence of sufficient funds for the
duration of your stay. Visas are not
required for citizens of Britain, Ireland,
Australia, New Zealand and the USA.
Visitors under 18 years of age
unaccompanied by an adult must carry
a letter from a parent or guardian
granting permission to travel in Canada.

Visitors are only allowed to work in
Canada if authorisation was obtained
prior to entry into the country.

Numerous international airlines serve
Vancouver with regularly scheduled
flights from Europe, Asia, the South
Pacific, the USA, Mexico and South
America. Vancouver International
Airport and Canada Customs and
Immigration can be very busy in
summer and at Christmas and Easter.

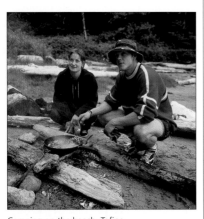
Camping on the beach, Tofino

Customs (*tel: (604) 666 0545*) and
immigration (*www.cic.gc.ca*) regulations
are strict, and baggage may be searched.
Fruit and animal products may not be
imported. There is no inbound duty-
free shop.

Vancouver Airport is a 30-minute
drive from downtown. Taxis from
Level II (Domestic Arrivals) cost about
C$20–30 to go downtown. Airporter
buses (*tel: (604) 946 8866, toll free (800)
668 3141; www.yvrairporter.com*) also
leave from Level II every 20 minutes and
stop at major downtown hotels and the
Greyhound Bus Depot. The cost is
about C$12 one way or C$18 round-trip
per person. Passengers en route to
Whistler can take the direct Perimeter's
Whistler Express bus (*tel: (604) 266
5386; www.perimeterbus.com*), and there
are also direct buses to White Rock,
Fraser Valley, Surrey (Century Valley
Airporter) and Victoria (Pacific Coach
Lines, *tel: 1 (800) 661 1725;
www.pacificcoach.com*).

Camping
Camping is a wonderful way to enjoy
the fresh air and natural beauty and to
make new friends, especially in summer.
There are hundreds of campsites
in BC, several of them in Greater
Vancouver. The Capilano RV
Campground (*tel: (604) 987 4722*), a
10-minute drive across the Lions Gate
Bridge from the city centre, is one of the
best urban camping areas in the world.
Suburban campsites include the
Burnaby Cariboo RV Park (*tel: (604)
420 1722, global toll free fax: (0800) 408*

55470; *www.bcrv.com*), Parks Canada RV Inn (*tel: (604) 943 5811; www.parkscanada.ca*) in Delta, Richmond RV Park (*tel: (604) 270 7878; www.welcometobc.ca/vancamping/*) and Peace Arch RV Park (*tel: (604) 594 7009; www.peacearchrvpark.com*) in Surrey. The campsite at Porteau Cove Provincial Park (*tel: (604) 986 9371*) overlooks Howe Sound, the most southerly fiord in North America.

Mountain Equipment Co-op (130 W Broadway; *tel: (604) 872 7858; www.mec.ca*) hires tents, camping equipment and other sporting goods.

For more information, pick up the *SuperCamping* booklet from any Travel InfoCentre, which lists private campsites, BC parks and RV and motorhome dealers.

Children

Vancouver is a great place for a family holiday (*see pp154–5*). Children love the spacious parks and playgrounds to romp and roam. Public transport, whether on planes, trains, buses or ferries, offers reduced fares for youngsters, who particularly enjoy roaming around the decks of the big BC ferries. Most Vancouver attractions offer reduced admission prices for children.

Many hotels make an extra effort to cater to children, with special menus, reduced room rates and other services. The Hyatt Regency (*tel: (800) 233 1234, toll free worldwide*) has its Camp Hyatt Passport (for kids aged three to 15) that offers puppet shows, films, arts and crafts and more.

For a list of special treats for kids, check *www.kidsvancouver.com* that lists

year-round and rainy-day things to do such as the Granville Island Museums (*tel: (604) 683 1939*) with their huge display of toy and model trains or special current events for kids. The Vancouver TouristInfo Centre also has its comprehensive *Kids' Guide to Vancouver*, and *Kids friendly! British Columbia* (*tel: (604) 541 6192; www.kidfriendly.org*) directs visitors to business and enterprises that are decidedly 'kid friendly.' HelloBC (*tel: toll free (800) 435 5622; www.hellobc.com*) is another good contact for rooting out children's activities.

In addition to museums, parks, aquatic centres and special indoor play areas, the city and neighbouring communities have a host of special events through the year including the Vancouver International Children's Festival each May. Playland, open from Easter throughout the summer, offers various historic sites and many splashdown parks and water slides. The Cloverdale Rodeo each Victoria Day is a huge attraction.

Climate

Compared with other cities in Canada, Vancouver and Victoria have a moderate climate, thanks in part to Pacific Ocean currents. There are few extremes in temperature. Vancouver's highest recorded temperature is 33°C (91°F) and the lowest is −18°C (0°F). But clouds and rain can be abundant, especially during the winter months of November, December and January. While about 100cm (39 inches) of rain fall on Vancouver Airport each year, some areas of the North Shore receive as much as 250cm (98 inches) annually. As a rule, the

Weather Conversion Chart
25.4mm = 1 inch
°F = 1.8 x °C + 32

summer months of June, July and August are the driest and sunniest. Monthly hours of sunshine average 305 in July and 44 in December. For a recorded weather report, call Environment Canada (*tel: (604) 664 9010*), which also predicts the possibility of rain.

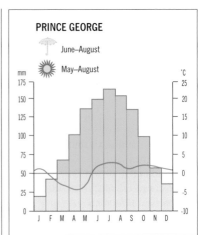

Consulates

Embassies are located in Ottawa,

Canada's capital, but among the consulates in Vancouver are the following:
Australia: *888 Dunsmuir Street. Tel: (604) 684 1177.*
New Zealand: *888 Dunsmuir Street. Tel: (604) 684 7388.*
UK: *1111 Melville Street. Tel: (604) 683 4421.*
United States: *1075 West Pender Street. Tel: (604) 685 4311.*

Crime

Vancouver is still a generally safe city, compared with such vast urban centres as London and New York. Downtown streets are well lit, but caution and common sense are good watchwords. Report any theft immediately to your hotel and the police.

Customs regulations

Duty-free allowances for visitors aged 19 and older are 200 cigarettes or 50 cigars or 1kg of tobacco, 1.14 litres of spirits or wine or 24 cans or bottles of beer or ale, and other dutiable goods up to a limit of C$200 in value. There is no duty on personal belongings for use during your visit. Gifts valued at more than C$60 are subject to duty and tax on the excess amount. Any currency carried worth C$10,000 or more must be declared. Revolvers, pistols and fully automatic firearms are prohibited entry into Canada. Quarantine regulations are strict. Plants must be declared and inspected by Agriculture Canada; animals may be quarantined for up to three months. The Customs website *www.cra-arc.gc.ca* provides full information.

Driving
Breakdowns

The BC Automobile Association (*tel: (604) 298 2122*) honours memberships of other automobile associations around the world. Any automobile club card is also valid for discounts at various hotels and attractions. Request the CAA discount when making reservations. For information on highway conditions, available for free, contact the *Talking Yellow Pages* (*Vancouver tel: (604) 299 6581 greater Vancouver area, (250) 861 2929 rest of BC; on Telus mobility, call *4997*). The service is available in most cities and towns in Canada. On the BC Highways website, webcam images show a continually updated image of highway conditions: *www.th.gov.bc.ca/bchighwaycam*

Conversion Table

FROM	TO	MULTIPLY BY
Inches	Centimetres	2.54
Feet	Metres	0.3048
Yards	Metres	0.9144
Miles	Kilometres	1.6090
Acres	Hectares	0.4047
Gallons	Litres	4.5460
Ounces	Grams	28.35
Pounds	Grams	453.6
Pounds	Kilograms	0.4536
Tons	Tonnes	1.0160

To convert back, for example from centimetres to inches, divide by the number in the third column.

Men's Suits

UK	36	38	40	42	44	46	48
Rest of Europe	46	48	50	52	54	56	58
USA/Canada	36	38	40	42	44	46	48

Dress Sizes

UK	8	10	12	14	16	18
France	36	38	40	42	44	46
Italy	38	40	42	44	46	48
Rest of Europe	34	36	38	40	42	44
USA/Canada	6	8	10	12	14	16

Men's Shirts

UK	14	14.5	15	15.5	16	16.5	17
Rest of Europe	36	37	38	39/40	41	42	43
USA/Canada	14	14.5	15	15.5	16	16.5	17

Men's Shoes

UK	7	7.5	8.5	9.5	10.5	11
Rest of Europe	41	42	43	44	45	46
USA/Canada	8	8.5	9.5	10.5	11.5	12

Women's Shoes

UK	4.5	5	5.5	6	6.5	7
Rest of Europe	38	38	39	39	40	41
USA/Canada	6	6.5	7	7.5	8	8.5

Car hire

Hiring a car is relatively inexpensive. Vehicles may be hired through Thomas Cook branches (*see p186*). Major car hire (rental) companies include:
Avis (*tel: (604) 606 2866*);
Budget (*tel: (604) 668 7000*);
Hertz (*tel: (604) 606 3782*);
National Car Rental
(*tel: (604) 207 3730*).
A major credit card is required to hire a car (otherwise a passport, a return ticket and a cash deposit), even if you plan to pay cash. The VISA Gold Card, among others, provides free car insurance; if you are planning to hire a car for a few weeks, it is worth investing in a gold credit card if you qualify. The minimum age to hire a car is 21.

The companies listed also hire campervans, motorhomes and four-wheel-drive vehicles. Chauffeured limousines and other vehicles are also available. For the budget-minded, try **Rent-A-Wreck** (*tel: (604) 688 0001*). Car-hire companies can charge double to fill up the tank, so it is better to do it yourself before returning the car. Remember to drive on the right in Canada.

Petrol

Petrol (gas) is sold by the litre in regular, premium or super grades, all unleaded, and is reasonably priced.

Electricity

Canada's electric current is an alternating 110–120 volts and 60 cycles. Adaptors are sold in some hotel shops and at Gulliver's Travels in Park Royal

(*tel: (604) 922 9650*) and the Sinclair shopping centres.

Emergency telephone numbers

Ambulance: *911* or *0* for operator.
Dental service: contact your hotel concierge for a recommendation.
Emotional Crisis Centre: *(604) 872 3311.*
Fire and rescue: *911* or *0* for operator.
Marine and Aircraft distress:
(*800*) *567 5111.*
MasterCard: *1 800 307 7309* (toll free) for loss or theft of cards.
Poison Control Centre: *(604) 682 5050.*
Police: *911* or *0* for operator.
Prescription Service: contact your hotel concierge; prescriptions are available only by visiting a Canadian physician.
RCMP Freeway Patrol: *911* or *0* for operator.
Thomas Cook traveller's cheque loss or theft: call *00 44 1733 318950* (*toll free*) to report lost or stolen cheques within 24 hours (*see also* Money matters, *p183*).

Health

No vaccinations are required for entry into Canada.

Tap water is usually safe to drink. Campers are advised to boil water from lakes and rivers. Canadian health-care standards are high. If you become ill, ask your hotel to recommend a nearby physician.

Medical insurance which should cover the duration of your stay in Canada is essential, as medical services are expensive. A visit to a general practitioner, or a stay in a hospital, could be a costly affair.

Hire facilities

Bicycles

Cycling around Stanley Park and other areas of Vancouver is a wonderful way to explore the city and enjoy the sights. Contact Spokes Bicycle Rentals (*tel: (604) 688 5141*) at the Georgia Street entrance to the park, or check the *Yellow Pages* of the telephone directory.

Boats

Sailing boats, motorboats and houseboats are available for hire from dozens of companies both in and outside Vancouver.

Contact the nearest Travel InfoCentre for details.

Hitchhiking

Hitchhiking is not illegal, indeed many backpackers do it, but it is not a recommended form of travel.

Insurance

Any medical, baggage or other personal insurance should be purchased before leaving home.

Any vehicle hire automatically includes third-party-liability insurance for damage to people and property.

Loss and damage insurance, which covers the hire car, costs extra, as do personal accident insurance and personal effects coverage for the driver and passengers.

Language

Canada has two official languages: English and French. English is the predominant language of BC. However, thanks to the native Indians and continuing waves of immigrants from Europe, Asia and around the world, many other languages, ranging from Chinook to Vietnamese, are also spoken. Canadian English has been most influenced by Americans, primarily through the media and advertising. Following are a few words familiar to British Columbians, but foreign to many visitors:

Anglophone	English-speaking person
bannock	Indian bread
bar	a ridge of sand or gravel in a stream or river where gold may be found by panning, but also a drinking place
First Nations	native Indian people
Inuit	Eskimo
Mountie	RCMP officer
potlatch	a native Indian festival
saltchuk	ocean

Lost property

Vancouver has two lost property centres: BC Transit (bus, SkyTrain losses) *tel: (604) 682 7887*, and Police (lost property rooms). Otherwise check with the nearest police station or call the head office of BC Transit.

Maps

Maps of Vancouver and BC are available from any Travel InfoCentre.

Media

Newspapers and magazines

The best daily in the country, the

morning *Globe & Mail*, has limited local news. However, *The Province* (*www.vancouverprovince.com*), a tabloid, and *The Vancouver Sun* (*www.vancouversun.com*), a broadsheet, both morning papers, cover city news and events. *The Georgia Strait* covers the Vancouver arts and entertainment scene. All three are available at news-stands and in street coin boxes. The weekly *Westender,* published on Thursdays, provides compact coverage of entertainment and other downtown and West End events, and is available free at most hotels. The monthly *WHERE Vancouver* is also available in hotels at no charge and for a dollar in coin boxes at the SeaBus Terminal. It is designed especially for visitors and includes information on shopping, dining, attractions, entertainment, special events, maps and evening television programmes.

For general information on what's on in Vancouver, visit the website *www.allianceforarts.com* (*hotline: (604) 684 2787*), *www.mybc.com,* or *www.showtimetickets.com* (*tel: (604) 688 5000 or toll-free (800) 480-SHOW*), an online ticket reservation service for concert or theatre events.

The Tourism Vancouver tourist information centre is at *Waterfront Centre, 200 Burrard Street* (*tel: (604) 682 2222; www.tourismvancouver.com*). Tourism BC (*tel: toll free 1 800 HELLO BC; www.hellobc.com*).

Radio and television
Favourite local radio stations include CBC at 690 AM and CKNW 980 (talk, music and sport); CHQM at 1320 AM (memory music); and 103.5 FM (contemporary music).

Local television stations include CBC-TV (Canadian Broadcasting Corporation) on Cable 3; BCTV (the CTV network) on Cable 11; and the Knowledge Network (the BC educational channel) on Cable 5 (no commercials). Dozens of other channels, including PBS, ABC, CBS and NBC from the USA, are also available locally. Check the listings at the back of *WHERE Vancouver* magazine.

Money matters
Currency
Canada has a decimal currency system with 100 cents to the dollar. Coins are one cent, five cents (a nickel), 10 cents (a dime), 25 cents (a quarter) and the one-dollar coin called a 'loonie' (because of the loon bird on one face). The bills (notes) are colour-coded: $5 is blue, $10 is purple, $20 is green, $50 is red, $100 is beige; $2 is now a coin called the 'twoonie'. Merchants seem reluctant to give up a lot of change, so $100-bills are not popular. $20-bills are always acceptable. Thomas Cook traveller's cheques denominated in Canadian or US dollars are a secure and convenient way of carrying larger amounts of money and can be used as cash in most hotels and restaurants.

Money exchange
Most foreign currencies and traveller's cheques can be exchanged at the foreign exchange counters at the airport, at all major city banks and hotels, and at all Thomas Cook Foreign Exchange locations, including the following: *Marlin Travel, Park Royal Shopping Centre, 2009 Park Royal South, West*

Vancouver, BC. Tel: (604) 922 9301;
Thomas Cook, Pacific Centre Mall, 777
Dunsmuir Street, Vancouver, BC. Tel:
(604) 684 3291;
Thomas Cook, Oakridge Centre, 419–650
West 41st Avenue, Vancouver, BC. Tel:
(604) 266 1712;
Marlin Travel, Richmond Centre, 6551
No 3 Road, Richmond, BC. Tel: (604) 273
8844;
Thomas Cook, Coquitlam Centre, 2929
Barnet Highway, Port Coquitlam, BC. Tel:
(604) 464 2133;
Thomas Cook, Guildford Town Centre,
Surrey, BC. Tel: (604) 584 3338;
Thomas Cook, Sussex Place, 1001 Douglas
Street, Victoria, BC. Tel: (250) 361 4115;
Thomas Cook, 4230 Gateway Drive,
Whistler, BC. Tel: (604) 938 0101.
These and other branches will cash
Thomas Cook traveller's cheques free
of commission and provide emergency
assistance in cases of loss or theft of
Thomas Cook traveller's cheques.

Since exchange rates fluctuate, check
the Canadian dollar rates upon your
arrival in Canada. Credit cards, such as
American Express, MasterCard and
VISA, are widely accepted.

If you need to transfer money
quickly, you can use the MoneyGram[SM]
Money transfer service. For more
details, call Freephone *0800 897198*
(in the UK).

Taxes
The federal GST (Goods and Services
Tax) is currently 7 per cent. However,
foreign visitors may claim a rebate when
purchases total more than C$100. Pick
up a rebate form at the nearest Travel
InfoCentre, or call toll free 1 800 668

4748 for further details. BC provincial
sales tax (exempt from children's
clothing and food) is 7 per cent on most
merchandise, hotel tax is 17 per cent
(including the 7 per cent GST), and
10 per cent is added to the price of
liquor consumed in bars and
restaurants.

National holidays
Banks, post offices, liquor stores,
government offices, most other offices
and many stores are closed on these
holidays. City buses, the SeaBus and the
SkyTrain operate on a reduced schedule.
Vancouver hotels are rarely fully booked
during Canadian holidays, but there are
seldom rooms available during
American holidays.

New Year's Day 1 January
Good Friday late March, early April
Easter late March, early April
Victoria Day 24 May or the preceding
    Monday
Canada Day 1 July
BC Day 1 August
Labour Day first Monday in
    September
Thanksgiving Day second Monday in
    October
Remembrance Day 11 November
Christmas Day 25 December
Boxing Day 26 December

Opening times
Banks Major banks downtown open at
8am. Some banks are open on Saturday
morning, but all are closed on Sundays
and holidays. Normal banking hours are
10am–4pm Monday to Friday, often
extending to 5pm on Friday.

Museums, galleries and attractions

Most are open daily 10am–5pm, but some are closed one day a week, and some have extended or shortened hours on certain days.

Post offices All post offices are open Monday to Friday 8.30am–5.30pm. Some sub-offices are open Saturday mornings, and postal counters in 7-Eleven stores are open until 11pm.

Shops Most shops and stores are open Monday to Friday 9.30am–6pm, with hours extended to 9pm on Thursday and Friday. Most are open Saturday 9.30am–5.30pm, and many are on Sunday, noon–5pm. Such convenience stores as 7-Eleven are often open 7am–11pm, and some are open all night.

Pharmacies

Medical prescriptions in BC are available only through a local physician. Many pharmacies are hidden at the back of big drugstores. These drugstores sell all kinds of non-prescription medicines, along with contraceptives, insect repellent, vitamins, tissues and a host of other items. Shoppers Drug Mart, at *1125 Davie Street (tel: (604) 669 2424)*, is open 24 hours a day, seven days a week. London Drugs, at *1187 Robson Street (tel: (604) 448 4819)*, is open from Monday to Saturday 9am–11pm and on Sunday 10am–10pm.

Photography

Print film, which is inexpensive and sold almost everywhere, can be developed within an hour or two at numerous photo shops. Slide film, sold primarily in photo shops, takes 24 hours to develop,

except for Kodachrome, which takes a week. Lens & Shutter, at *700 Dunsmuir Street (tel: (604) 684 4422)*, provides a reliable service for both prints and slides. Many shops sell disposable cameras.

Places of worship

Places of worship representing various denominations and faiths in and around Vancouver include:

Akali Singh Sikh Temple
1890 Skeena St. Tel: (604) 254 2117.
Beth Israel Synagogue
4350 Oak St. Tel: (604) 731 4161.
Canadian Memorial United Church
1825 W 16th Ave. Tel: (604) 731 3101.
Central Presbyterian Church
1155 Thurlow St. Tel: (604) 683 1913.
Christ Church Anglican Cathedral
690 Burrard St. Tel: (604) 682 3848.
Christian Science Church
1900 W 12th Ave. Tel: (604) 733 8040.
First Baptist Church
969 Burrard St. Tel: (604) 683 8441.
Holy Rosary Catholic Cathedral
646 Richards St. Tel: (604) 682 6774.
Ismaili Mosque
4010 Canada Way, Burnaby.
Tel: (604) 438 4010.

Police

The RCMP (Royal Canadian Mounted Police) cover areas where there is no municipal police force. Call *911* or *0* for the operator for any emergencies.

Post offices

The main post office at 349 West Georgia Street is open from Monday to Friday 8.30am–5.30pm. Many sub-offices in malls, drugstores, convenience stores and even dry-cleaning shops are also open on Saturday as well. Most offer postage, courier and facsimile (fax) services. Canada Post boxes are red. Mail can be received 'c/o General Delivery' at any post office in Canada. To send a telegram, contact Canada Post.

Senior citizens

Numerous transport and tour companies, hotels, stores, attractions and events offer reduced rates to people as young as 50. Carry an ID card or any other official document that indicates your birth date.

The Hyatt, Park Royal and Westin Bayshore hotels, among others, offer senior discounts. Many local restaurants give 10 to 20 per cent discount to seniors, while others offer small-portion meals and early-bird specials – enquire upon entering any restaurant.

Domestic airlines, the harbour and Granville Island ferries, city transport including the SeaBus and SkyTrain all offer reduced fares to seniors. Call the company directly for details. Such attractions as the Vancouver Aquarium, the Dr Sun Yat-Sen Chinese Garden, the Vancouver Art Gallery, the Museum of Anthropology, the Maritime Museum, Science World, the IMAX show, the Bloedel Conservatory and Grouse Mountain offer reduced admission prices to seniors. The Vancouver Aquatic Centre offers a seniors' programme which includes exercises on the deck and in the pool, and organises day trips outside the city, and such special events as Valentine Tea.

City cinemas, theatres and the symphony offer reduced rates to seniors, sometimes by as much as 50 per cent. Some supermarkets, drugstores and

department stores reduce prices by 10 to 15 per cent one day a month for seniors.

Travel-wise seniors get great holiday bargains through Elderhostel at *33 Prince Arthur Avenue, Toronto, Ontario M5R 1B2*. A monthly publication, *The Independent Times* (*tel: (604) 580 1844*), is geared to the needs of senior readers and can be found at Shoppers Drug Mart or some banks and travel information centres in season.

Student and youth travel

Many attractions and events in the Vancouver area offer reduced rates for students. Bring your student card.

Sustainable tourism

Thomas Cook is a strong advocate of ethical and fairly traded tourism and believes that the travel experience should be as good for the places visited as it is for the people who visit them. That's why we firmly support The Travel Foundation, a charity that develops solutions to help improve and protect holiday destinations, their environment, traditions and culture. To find out what you can do to make a positive difference to the places you travel to and the people who live there, please visit *www.thetravelfoundation.org.uk*

Telephones

Public telephones can be found in post offices, hotel lobbies, public buildings, and in phone booths on various streets throughout the city. Local calls cost 25 cents for an unlimited time. Some public phones are specifically for long-distance calls and some are designated for credit card use only. Both local and international calls are usually more expensive on hotel phones. Inexpensive long-distance phonecards are available under a variety of names and can be purchased at post offices and a variety of other stores. Call 0 for the operator to enquire about discounts for dialling both domestically and abroad at certain times. The area codes for BC are 604 for the lower mainland to Hope and north to Whistler, and 250 for the rest of the province.

International calls can be dialled direct using the following codes: Britain is 011 +44 + city code minus the initial 0 + number, Australia 011 +61 + city code + number, and New Zealand 011 +64 + city code + number. For calls to other provinces of Canada and to the USA, dial 1, the area code and the number.

Thomas Cook

Thomas Cook Travel can book items such as sightseeing tours and car hire. For a list of the branches most likely to be used by incoming travellers, *see* Money exchange *p183*.

Ticket agencies

For such events as opera, symphony, ballet, theatre, sports, rock concerts and some attractions, call Ticketmaster on *(604) 280 4444*. By telephone you can pay by American Express, MasterCard or VISA, while at counters scattered throughout city shopping malls, you can pay either by credit card or cash. Cinema tickets are, however, sold only at individual theatres. For programme times at Cineplex Odeon, you should check *www.cineplex.com*

Time

Most of BC is on Pacific Standard Time, which in summer is nine hours behind GMT. Clocks are put back an hour on the last Sunday in October, and an hour forward on the first Sunday in April, for daylight-saving time. Vancouver time is the same as California, three hours behind Toronto and New York. For most of the year, Vancouver is 18 hours behind Sydney and 21 hours behind Auckland.

Tipping

Tips generally range from 10 to 20 per cent in restaurants and bars, and for taxis. Tipping is optional for porters, doormen, chambermaids and other service personnel.

Toilets

Public toilets are found in railway and bus terminals, shopping centres and department stores. A hotel or restaurant will sometimes let you use its facilities.

Tourist offices

For maps and brochures on Vancouver and BC, contact:
Tourism BC. *PO Box 9830, 1 Stn. A, Prov. Govt., Victoria BC V8W 9W5. Tel: (800) HelloBC toll free; or (604) HelloBC; www.HelloBC.com*

Tours

UK-based travellers can pre-book a range of tours and travel options at advantageous rates when arranging their trip with Thomas Cook Holidays (details from any branch of Thomas Cook, or if in the UK by telephoning *01733 417000*). Visitors to Vancouver can take to the water aboard the SeaBus or the Granville Island and BC ferries, in a canoe or kayak, or on a motorboat or yacht. Landlubbers can tour on foot and by bicycle, antique car, bus, train or limousine. Some visitors take to the air in seaplanes, gliders, helicopters and hot-air balloons. Although North American travellers tend to be do-it-yourself sightseers or rely on friends and relatives, numerous commercial tours are available, especially in summer. Many can be pre-booked within your overall travel plan, or booked at the Thomas Cook Travel offices listed above and on pp182–3. The booklet *Official Visitors Guide*, stocked at Travel InfoCentres, is helpful (and can also be requested through *www.tourismvancouver.com* or *www.hellobc.com*).

Bicycle tours

Cycling BC (*332–1367 W. Broadway. Tel: (604) 737 3034; www.cycling.bc.ca*) is the umbrella organisation for several cycling clubs, including the Vancouver Bike Club which welcomes non-members to join in city cycling and tours further afield for both leisurely wheeling and technical training camps.

Bus and car tours

Gray Line (*tel: (604) 879 9287*) and Pacific Coach Lines (*tel: (604) 662 7575*) among others, offer various sightseeing tours, with itineraries ranging from a city circle, similar to the Trolley tour (*see pp36–7*), and an evening dinner tour (a great way to meet fellow travellers), to a seven-day return ride through the Rockies to Calgary. Early Motion Tours (*tel: (604) 687 5088*) offer the luxury of a

finely tuned original 1928 or 1930 Model A Ford phaeton convertible. The driver, former teacher called 'Fridge' Fridulin, provides a continuous commentary on city sights and a Polaroid photograph of you and the phaeton as a souvenir. Limojet Gold (*tel: (604) 273 1331; toll free (800) 278 8742; www.limojetgold.com*) creates tailored tours in the luxury of a limousine, day or night, in addition to airport and intercity transfer.

Historical walking tours

Local historian Chuck Davis (*tel: (604) 583 2920*), who probably knows Vancouver past and present better than anyone, designs walking tours of the city centre to meet your requirements.

Water tours

Gray Line (*tel: (604) 879 9287*) and the SS *Beaver* (*tel: N113040 on Van 25; marine radio via the 'O' operator*) offer harbour sightseeing excursions. The SS *Beaver* tour of Indian Arm includes a mesquite-grilled salmon lunch. Both Gray Line and the SS *Beaver*, along with Bayshore Yacht Charters (*tel: (604) 691 6936*), offer three-hour dinner cruises. Sewell's Landing Marina (*tel: (604) 921 3474*) in Horseshoe Bay offers skippered fishing tours. For white-water rafting from May to September, contact Hyak Wilderness Adventures (*tel: (604) 734 8622*), who guided staff of the *National Geographic* down the Chilko and Chilcotin rivers. The company's shuttle service runs from downtown Vancouver to the Chilliwack, Thompson and Chilko rivers.

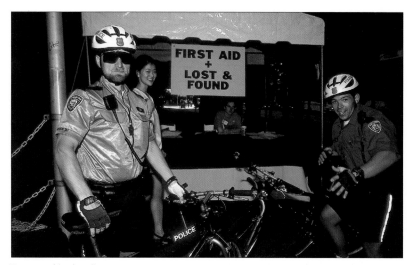

Vancouver bicycle police

Transport
Airlines
Air BC & Air Canada (*tel: 1 888 247 2262; www.aircanada.com*)
Harbour Air (*tel: (604) 274 1277; toll free (800) 665; www.harbour-air.com*)
Helijet Airways (*tel: (604) 273 4688; www.helijet.com*)
West Jet Airlines (*tel: 1 888 WEST JET; www.westjet.com*)

Buses
Airport Express (*tel: (604) 946 8866; www.yvrairporter.com*) operates between the airport and downtown.
Gray Line (*tel: (604) 879 5088; www.graylinewest.com*) offers sightseeing tours.
Greyhound (*tel: (604) 482 8747; toll free (800) 328 9093; www.greyhound.ca*) operates throughout Canada.
Maverick Coach Lines (*tel: (604) 255 1171; www.maverickcoachlines.bc.ca*) runs to Whistler.

BC Transit (*tel: (604) 453 4500; www.bctransit.com*), Vancouver's regional public transport system, includes buses, the SeaBus and the SkyTrain, which run along major arteries through the city centre and suburbs. There are three fare zones in Greater Vancouver. Day passes are available for children, adults and senior citizens. Exact change in coins is preferred, but tickets and passes are sold at 7-Eleven and other stores.

Transit timetables are available from public libraries, city and municipal halls, Travel InfoCentres and BC Transit offices and terminals. For Blue Bus routes and schedules from downtown to West Vancouver, call *(604) 985 7777*.

The SeaBuses, which are actually 400-passenger catamaran ferries, make the 15-minute trip across Burrard Inlet to North Vancouver every 15 minutes. The SkyTrain (*tel: (604) 520 3641*) runs 28km from Canada Place downtown to King George Station, beyond New Westminster, with 15 stops en route. Trains run every 3–5 minutes at an average speed of 75km per hour (47 mph).

Ferries
The little Aquabus Ferries operating from the foot of Hornby Street, and the False Creek ferries from the Aquatic Centre, make the five-minute run to and from Granville Island all year round. BC Ferries (*tel: 1 888 223 3779*) carry both vehicles and foot passengers and run from Tsawwassen (an hour's drive south from the city centre) to Swartz Bay (a half-hour from Victoria) and Nanaimo on Vancouver Island, and to the Gulf Islands. From Horseshoe Bay (a half-hour drive northwest from downtown Vancouver), ferries sail regularly to Nanaimo, Bowen Island and the Sunshine Coast.

Taxis
It is hard to hail a cab in downtown Vancouver, especially in the pouring rain when you need one most. It is best to head to the nearest big hotel, where taxis usually wait in line, or to call one of the following cab companies:
Black Top (*tel: (604) 683 4567 or (604) 731 1111*).
Yellow Cab (*tel: (604) 681 1111 or (604) 876 5555*).

Trains
VIA Rail (*tel: (888) 842 7245; www.viarail.ca*) operates a thrice-weekly passenger service across Canada, departing from the station on Main Street opposite Science World. VIA Rail's luxury trans-Canadian train, the *Silver and Blue*, runs from Toronto to Vancouver and can be booked outside Canada. So can the privately run Rocky Mountaineer Vacations, running from Vancouver through Jasper and Banff to Calgary.

Summer tours with Rocky Mountaineer Vacations (*tel: (604) 606 7245; www.rockymountaineer.com*) from Vancouver to Banff and Jasper are especially popular. Details of local rail, bus and ferry services are shown in the *Thomas Cook Overseas Timetable*, which is available to buy online from *www.thomascookpublishing.com*, from Thomas Cook branches in the UK or by phoning *01733 416477*.

Travellers with disabilities
Most major hotels and attractions in Vancouver are wheelchair-accessible. For information on facilities for people with physical disabilities, contact any Travel InfoCentre, or the Community Resources Consultant at the Canadian Paraplegic Association, at 780 Southwest Marine Drive, BC V6P 5Y7 (*tel: (604) 324 3611*).

The Vancouver Trolley Company

ACKNOWLEDGEMENTS
Thomas Cook Publishing wishes to thank HELENA ZUKOWSKI for the photographs reproduced in this book, to whom the copyright belongs, with the exception of the following:

AQUASHACK DIVING SERVICE: page 108
GRAHAM OSBORNE/VANCOUVER, COAST & MOUNTAINS TOURISM: page 125
LADY ROSE MARINE SERVICES: pages 118a, 118b, 119a, 119b
CHRIS POTTER: pages 14, 88, 121
RICHARD SHAPKA: pages 32b, 51, 53, 55, 66, 77a, 77b, 88, 90, 91, 110, 149, 153
ROY STEWART: pages 56, 57, 67, 68, 83
MUSEUM OF ANTHROPOLOGY (all photos BILL MCLENNAN): pages 38 (*The Raven and the First Men* by Bill Reid, 1980), 58, 59
VANCOUVER AQUARIUM (photo DIANE MORRISON): page 72
GROUSE MOUNTAIN RESORT: pages 80, 82, 158
OCEANSIDE TOURISM ASSOCIATION: page 112
CARIBOO CHILCOTIN COAST TOURISM: page 130
BARD ON THE BEACH: page 151
JEFF VINNICK/VANCOUVER CANUCKS: page 163
TOURISM WHISTLER: pages 84 (John Henebry), 85 (Fairmont Chateau Whistler)

Index: MARIE LORIMER

Proof-reading: JAN McCANN for CAMBRIDGE PUBLISHING MANAGEMENT LTD

Send your thoughts to
books@thomascook.com

We're committed to providing the very best up-to-date information in our travel guides and constantly strive to make them as useful as they can be. You can help us to improve future editions by letting us have your feedback. If you've made a wonderful discovery on your travels that we don't already feature, if you'd like to inform us about recent changes to anything that we do include, or if you simply want to let us know your thoughts about this guidebook and how we can make it even better – we'd love to hear from you.

Send us ideas, discoveries and recommendations today and then look out for your valuable input in the next edition of this title. And, as an extra 'thank you' from Thomas Cook Publishing, you'll be automatically entered into our exciting monthly prize draw.

Emails to the above address, or letters to Travellers Project Editor, Thomas Cook Publishing, PO Box 227, Unit 18, Coningsby Road, Peterborough PE3 8SB, UK.

Please don't forget to let us know which title your feedback refers to!